THE FIFTH DIMENSION

WHAT PEOPLE ARE SAYING ABOUT
THE FIFTH DIMENSION

Every now and then, a book comes along that can redefine your future and reshape your destiny. *The Fifth Dimension* is one of those books. My friend, Dr. Charles Olmeda, has absolutely hit a home run with his latest masterpiece. In his writings, you will discover a fresh new perspective that will help you unleash your potential and bring reality to your dreams. His unparalleled insights throughout each page will give you the encouragement and direction you need to breathe new vision into your life. Do yourself a favor and read this book from cover to cover. It is an absolute game changer!

—Chris Sonksen
Pastor/Speaker/Author

In *The Fifth Dimension*, Dr. Charles Olmeda offers a transformative guide filled with deep spiritual wisdom. The book provides a profound understanding of life's dimensions, aiding personal and spiritual growth. In a poignant chapter, the author recounts feeling lost despite doing everything right, only to find motivation by recognizing his current position and destination. This insight emphasizes perseverance and finding direction in tough times. Through biblical narratives and practical advice, the book will help you navigate challenges, build resilience, and stay true to your dreams to ultimately deepen your faith and empower you to live a fulfilling, purposeful life.

—Dr. Debra J. Dean
Author, Speaker, Professor, Leadership Consultant

Imagine living in a body full of energy, a mind full of enthusiasm, and a future full of hope. This spectacular book by Dr. Charles Olmeda shows the clear path to living life on purpose to fulfill God's plans for you. This book is a must-read! Your great, great-grandchildren just may benefit from what you learn.

—Randy Detrick
Author
President, Blue Ridge Winery

Countless books have been written on the subject of divine guidance, often with overused slogans and outdated illustrations. Dr. Olmeda's book, *The Fifth Dimension*, offers a fresh approach to a timeless topic. This book will inspire you—and stretch you—to be more like Jesus.

—Hal Donaldson
President, Convoy of Hope

In *The Fifth Dimension*, Dr. Charles Olmeda offers a transformative framework for understanding personal growth through a five-dimensional model of life progression. This engaging work weaves biblical narratives with contemporary insights, encouraging readers to view success as a cyclical journey to be undertaken. For those willing to engage deeply with its principles, this book has the potential to be a transformative force, reshaping perspectives and reigniting dormant dreams.

—Eddie Rentz
Church Network Director, Convoy of Hope
Former National Youth Director, Assemblies of God

Dr. Olmeda has captured something fresh and thought-provoking in his book, *The Fifth Dimension*. Get ready to dream bigger and live better after reading through chapter after chapter of insightful challenges.

—Dr. Nick Garza
Network Area Director, Convoy of Hope

This is beyond a must-read. Without a doubt, this book, narrative, instruction manual, spiritual GPS, is a must-do!

—Samuel Rodriguez, Jr.
Executive Movie Producer, National Best-Selling Author
President, NHCLC

Dr. Charles Olmeda has written a must-read resource book for anyone considering the ministry or beyond. In *The Fifth Dimension*, Dr. Olmeda walks you through the five dimensions as he mentions and models them step-by-step. His experiences, backed by biblical parallels, will help you not just dream but see and live those dreams out to the fullest potential. Read this book and learn from a lead pastor who is living out the purposes of God in his life.

—Rev. Manuel A. Alvarez
Spanish Eastern District A/G, Superintendent
Executive Presbyter U.S.A.

THE FIFTH DIMENSION

UNVEILING THE PATH TO FULFILLMENT AND BEYOND

N. CHARLES OLMEDA, PH.D.

AVAIL

This book is dedicated to those who have been waiting, waiting, and waiting to see the fulfillment of God-size dreams become a realization. For those who have patiently waited to live in the fullness of a God-size vision—this one is for you! Let me remind you that the fulfillment of God-size dreams will always exceed your expectations. Hang tight, delay is not denial!

It is also dedicated to a God-sent mother, who left me too soon (at least from my human perspective), yet she believed and prayed for this underdog through a Christ-centered journey and into the fulfillment of God's will for his life. Though you will not see or read the book, I long for the day we see the ultimate fulfillment of God's dream—eternity in Heaven. Until we meet again!

CONTENTS

FOREWORD

"Today's complacency is tomorrow's captivity." This declaration sets the stage for the journey of discovery outlined in this book. When we push back against complacency, we embark on a path that reveals our purpose, passion, and the promises life holds. These revelations often come not through grandiose events but through subtle, challenging moments that define us.

In this narrative, my brother and friend, Dr. Charles Olmeda, offers a compelling exploration of such defining moments, inviting readers to reflect on their own life's journey. One memorable story that Olmeda shares is about a seemingly simple trip to New York City, which turned into a metaphorical journey of being lost and found, highlighting the spiritual realities of direction and purpose.

Olmeda recounts getting lost while trying to find a parking garage on a cold winter night in New York City. This experience serves as a poignant metaphor for the times we find ourselves without direction, unsure of our path or purpose. It is in these moments of uncertainty that we are called to pause, reflect, and discover the deeper truths of our lives.

The book delves into the concept of self-discovery, emphasizing that this journey can only truly begin within the context of the finished work of Jesus Christ. Olmeda explores how understanding who God is, who we are in Him, and our God-ordained purpose forms the foundation for spiritual, physical, mental, and emotional growth. This journey is not merely about personal fulfillment but also about fulfilling our divine calling to impact the world.

The narrative introduces the idea of the "fifth dimension," representing different stages of growth and understanding in our lives. It highlights the reality of a journey where there are seasons of preparation, pruning, and preservation by God. These dimensions challenge readers to examine their current state and encourage deeper introspection that can lead to transformative change. The journey through these stages is marked by God's grace and guidance, helping us to navigate life's challenges and celebrate its triumphs.

In essence, this narrative is a call to action. It encourages us to resist the temptation of complacency, seek a deeper understanding of our life's purpose, and embrace the journey of faith with renewed passion and commitment. Every setback or moment of confusion is not an end but a stepping stone toward fulfilling God's plan for our lives.

As you engage with this book, I encourage you to reflect deeply on the experiences shared, journal your thoughts, and use Olmeda's insights to navigate your unique journey. This journey is not just about reaching a destination but about embracing the transformative process, guided by faith in Jesus Christ.

May this book inspire you to push back against complacency, discover your divine purpose, and live out your calling with passion and conviction as you journey through the deeper, more meaningful dimensions of life.

—*Samuel Rodriguez*
New Season-Lead Pastor, NHCLC President/CEO
Author of Your Mess, God's Miracle!
Exec. Producer of "Breakthrough" and "Flamin' Hot" Movies

ACKNOWLEDGMENTS

First and foremost, thank you to my Lord and Savior, Jesus Christ, who paved the way and appointed me that I may "go forth and bear fruit—fruit that will last" (John 15:16). I would not be here without Your embedded dreams in my life! May I live to honor you!

Proverbs 18:22 says that "he who finds a wife finds a good thing and obtains favor from the LORD" (NRSV). Thank you, Reina—you are the epitome of that text. Thank you for believing in my dreams and picking up so many responsibilities, especially toward the end of my manuscript journey. You truly are the MVP. I love you to eternity! To my two daughters, Amberly and Andrea, you have been Daddy's biggest fans. You are a gift from God! This one's for you! May my life be only a taste of the greater things God will do in and through you!

The AVAIL team (Debbie, Sarah, Allison, Noah, and those behind the scenes)—your excellent spirit shines through in all you do. Dr. Megan Adelson, your author coaching and editing expertise is both scholarly and commendable. Thank you for making this project your own throughout the journey and for believing I could get this done within such time constraints. Martijn van Tilborgh, thank you for believing in the project and being a conduit through which many will be encouraged to dream God-size dreams. Andrew van Tilborgh, your photography expertise made me look better than I deserve. You're a genius. Thank you.

To my Transformation Church, LV family, thank you for your patience during this journey and for serving as the proverbial guinea pigs for my writing content. I could not have asked for a greater leadership and body of believers! To my two key office staff support systems, Cindy and Amberly—thank you for going beyond your call of duty. What would I do without you? To my newest IT guru, Jason Velazquez, your heart for serving is a gift. Thank you for all you do. Finally, thank you to all of my family, near and far, especially my dad, Alejandro Olmeda, and siblings—Nancy, Yisell, and Steven—who believed that "Charlie" could break past any limitation. In that vein, thank you to Rev. Samuel Rodriguez for setting the dream bar pretty high, for believing in this project, and for writing my foreword. Tuti (Elizabeth) and Grandpa (Samuel), your unconditional love makes me feel like I have two more parents; Lydia Lizzette, your love for academia has been contagious and your impact immeasurable; and to the Olmeda/Rodriguez familia, life is so much fun with you! Thank you for cheering from the sidelines!

"If you don't know where you're going,
whenever you get there is okay...."
—Author Unknown

INTRODUCTION

O ne of the worst feelings in life is not knowing where you are.
I remember one specific occasion where the frustrating,
emotional instability of hopelessness was so overwhelming that I
could scream. Let me explain.

Winters in the Northeast can be brutal. I remember one of those
brutal winter days at the age of seventeen or eighteen. I had decided
to treat myself and a friend to a theatrical experience on Broadway
in New York City. The temperature, if I remember correctly, must
have been about five degrees Fahrenheit. There is something
about New York City on a cold December evening that is sure to
take your breath away. The lights, décor, gigantic lit snowflakes
blanketing the front of corporate buildings, the holiday hustle and
bustle, and people skating at Rockefeller Center all make for a
winter-painting-over-the-fireplace-mantle type of setting. Though
I was born and raised in the Northeast, just a tunnel crossing away

from the Big Apple, breathing in the city air during the holidays never gets old.

Traveling into New York City on a Friday night is madness. Somehow, though I should have known better, I managed to travel into the city with very little time to spare before the opening curtain. It wasn't the first time I'd made this mistake. (It seems there are some lessons we just never learn.)

As you can imagine, several problems emerge with this type of mistake. For one, traffic is always unpredictable. Therefore, it is very likely you will miss the beginning of a show that you invested a few hundred dollars in. Secondly, you tend to spend more when you are pressed for time—this was certainly the case in my desperation to find parking in the Big Apple, particularly around the main venues. Such was my experience that cold winter Friday night.

Finding the right theater was not a problem. Finding a place to park without "breaking the bank" was another story. Tardiness had a price of its own as I frantically searched for the first and closest place I could park: a public parking garage about two-and-a-half blocks away from the venue. In retrospect, I realize the challenge is that the same corporate entity seems to manage most of the parking garages in the area. They all appear to bear the same colors and market the same complex pricing structures that would lead you to believe you need a doctoral degree in code deciphering methodology just to figure out what you will have to pay.

I pulled into the parking garage, cognizant of the limited time I had to find my seat in an already crowded theater. I proceeded to exit the parking garage and asked the first employee I saw to point me in the direction of the venue. If you ask my wife, that by itself is a miracle. The popular perception is that most men do not ask for directions. I was proving that theory wrong (at least for now). The employee pointed me in the direction I needed to walk, and off to the theater I went.

Unfortunately for me, the experience was not all I expected it to be. At that point, I was not sure whether I was frustrated that I had rushed and worried for no reason or whether I was simply glad the show was over. Who knows, maybe I was just tired from a long arduous week and the show was not to blame. Regardless, about two-and-a-half hours after entering, we gathered our belongings, put on our winter garb, and off to our car we went.

We left the building and began to follow our path back to the parking garage. We traveled the right number of blocks and made the right number of turns. (Keep in mind that at that point, it felt like below zero degrees Fahrenheit.) Finally, the parking garage. But wait! Though the parking garage had the same colors and the same complex pricing signs, the entrance to the garage was different. You drove straight into the entrance of this parking garage. We had parked in one with a steep slope you had to drive down to get to the attendant's window. How could this be? We retraced our steps back to the venue, looked at the building, and proceeded to journey back to where we thought the car was parked. No steep slope, and therefore, no car. Finally, it occurred to me to look at the back of the parking ticket stub for a printed address. To my surprise, lo and behold, there was an address. (There go the points I earned earlier for asking for directions.)

Learning quickly from this mistake, I asked for directions to the right parking garage. It had been about an hour since we had left the venue. I felt like frostbite was starting to settle in, and my friend's nagging about my poor sense of direction was not helping much.

It wasn't until I was one block away from the parking garage (one New York City block for those of you who are familiar) that I realized the theater had two identical entrances—one on either side of the building. Because I assumed I knew where I was going, I didn't realize that I was walking in the wrong direction.

It was frustrating to be not only unfamiliar with where I was but also to have endured undue stress, wasted time, and faded memories of what was a semi-decent theatrical experience. The only memorable experience that remains from that night—so much so that I am recounting it thirty-plus years later—was the mental anguish of thinking I knew where I was while unable to reach my destination.

> ### Never live in such a rush that you can't take time to determine where you are.

Isn't that like our lives? We think we are headed in the right direction and then something happens that causes us to feel lost. You will soon learn throughout this book that misconstruing the dimensions you are living out can cause you to feel frustrated and confused. If you don't recognize the next dimension looming on the horizon, you may be tempted to throw in the proverbial towel and quit before you see the fulfillment of your dreams.

I learned one extremely valuable lesson that night in New York City: never live in such a rush that you can't take time to determine where you are. I'm not only referring to a general space but the precise dimension you are in. It may not be where you want to be, but it can help you determine which way you need to go.

I don't pretend to have all the answers for you regarding where you are in life. But this I will tell you: whether you are an entrepreneur or a stay-at-home mom, a minister, priest or lay worker, a professor or a Hollywood star, the President of the United States, or Prime Time television's most popular host—or anyone else attracted by the title or contents of this book—you will or have experienced the cycle of life detailed throughout the next few chapters. That is, whether you have noticed it or not, or whether you can admit it or not, our life is not linear. There are moments, seasons, and dimensions that you must go through before you can see the fulfillment of your God-size dream or your God-size vision.

THE CYCLE BEGINS

Have you had successes in your life? They don't have to be grand by the standards of those you may feel have accomplished greater things. They could be as simple as making a team you thought you would never make or performing better than you thought you would. Perhaps you are looking at where you are in your career and thinking, *How did I ever make it this far?* Perhaps a thought, an idea, or a dream you once had has turned into something greater than you ever expected. If so, each dimension within the cycle of life laid out in this book will become very familiar. You will soon be able to identify a time in your life when you have walked through each dimension and recall the impact of that time on future experiences.

Maybe you are on the opposite side of the spectrum. You tried out for the team time and time again, only to be turned away. You find yourself struggling to find your place, like the right career in a dog-eat-dog society. You may be wondering, *When will I experience the FULL essence of what I have thus far only experienced in bits and pieces? When will I remain in a joyful season of life long enough without something falling apart?* You may have had dreams that have only ended in failures and hopes that have only brought betrayal. Breathe! This book is for you!

Like me, lost in New York City, you may be just one 180-degree turn from finding your destination. One moment, you may feel cold, lost, and frustrated, feeling like you will never arrive. The next moment, you may be sitting in the warmth of the very vehicle that will take you wherever you need to go. One moment, you may feel like you've made the biggest mistake of your life, and the next moment, you muse, *How did it all turn around in my favor?* One moment, you may feel betrayed, abandoned, and alone, feeling like no one understands your dreams while you invest in others with nothing to show for it. The next moment, you're basking in the fullness of what once was only a dream.

WHAT IF

What do you dream about? No, I don't mean the crazy all-over-the-place kind of dreams you dream because you stayed up late eating pizza. What do you really dream about? Where do you see yourself? What do you envision? That thing that, at times, becomes so real within that if you didn't know any better, you could almost taste it, smell it, touch it, hear it, or see it, only to then realize it was only a dream (or a vision).

What if I told you that some of those very dreams you dream and those visions you see have already been declared by God as reality?

Would you believe me? You don't have to. However, throughout this book, I will walk you through understanding five dimensions that you either have gone through or will go through in this journey we all call life. By the end of the fifth dimension, you be the judge. You determine the credibility of my suggestion. At the end of this journey, you can decide whether you have been living out God's purpose for your life or whether the storms of life have hit you so hard that you have lost your place. You decide whether those dreams and visions will remain just that—dreams and visions—or whether they will become a living reality.

Like my episode in New York City on that brutally cold evening, you may be asking, *If I am doing all the right things, then why do I feel so lost?* Like me, as I confronted some of the more challenging seasons of my life, you may be asking yourself, *Are the best years of my life over? Is this all there is? Am I crazy for dreaming so big when my "reality" says otherwise?* It wasn't until I realized exactly where I was that I found the energy I needed to make it to my destination. Even while I trekked the cold streets of New York, shivering and upset about lost time, something inside me rejoiced because I knew where I was headed. I had come to grips with my mistake and knew that my destination was near. I wasn't there yet, but by simply recognizing where I was, I had gotten a taste of what was to come. That was enough motivation to keep me going.

DIMENSIONS

The *Merriam-Webster Dictionary* defines dimensions, in part, as, "A level of existence or consciousness."[1]

---

1 *Merriam-Webster Dictionary*, s.v. "dimensions," http://www.merriam-webster.com/dictionary/dimension.

Remember my question about your ability to dream? Now imagine being able to live in a "dimension," a level of existence where those dreams—those visions—are tangible. Imagine a place where those deeply embedded promises you have sensed and felt are not simply a place you mentally visit, only to then face reality. Instead, it becomes a place of existence, a dwelling place.

No, this is not some New Age or name-it-claim-it theology geared at getting you excited about what is to come for your life. This goes deeper. This book is about your God-given assignment. This book is about living in the "fullness" of God for your life. This book is about knowing the cycle of life you *must* and *will* go through to live your life with purpose and on purpose.

Throughout the next five sections (or dimensions, as I categorically name them), I illustrate, simply for the sake of understanding, the five dimensions in the form of steps. I demonstrate the idea of moving forward and upward from one dimension to another. However, as we come to the end of the *fifth dimension*, I will illustrate the full cycle of what I consider to be *the fifth dimension model*. The illustration will undoubtedly put into perspective the cycle of life we are all exposed to.

WHAT TO EXPECT

My life, including how the revelation and material for this book came into existence, is part of the journey. Over the course of this book, you will read about *five dimensions*. (I will go deeper in chapter 1 about the meaning of this.)

This book is laid out in five different sections (dimensions)—one section per dimension. Each is then composed of five chapters. Each chapter will deal with the important aspects of each dimension.

To get the most out of this book, I encourage you to work through the companion study guide (see the QR code on the back of the book). The study guide will pose key reflection points that will prompt you to stop, reflect, journal, and allow God to help you with your self-analysis. As you work through the questions, ask yourself, *Is this the dimension I find myself in? What chapter can I relate to the most, and why?* There is something powerful and, at times, liberating about taking the thoughts and emotions you wrestle with and putting them on paper. It is like stepping outside of yourself for a moment and looking from the outside in. What do you see? Does it bring satisfaction? Does it stir feelings of regret? Do you notice things you never noticed before? If you haven't tried it, try it now. You will be amazed at what you learn about yourself. If you are to live in a dimension of fullness (I'm giving you a little taste of what's to come), then you will need to know someone better than you know anyone else. . . . and that person is you.

So, I invite you on this journey as we make our way to the *Fifth Dimension!*

IST DIMENSION
DREAMS & VISIONS

DREAMS
&
VISIONS

.

1

WHERE IT ALL BEGINS

"Yesterday is but today's memory, and tomorrow is today's dream."
—Khalil Gibran

"You have to dream before your dreams can come true."
—Abdul Kalam

"Now Joseph had a dream, and he told it to his brothers; and they hated him even more."
—Genesis 37:5 (NKJV)

I am fully aware that many classify dreams and visions as two different categories—a dream happens during sleep; a vision happens when we are awake. I am sure that if you researched the difference between the two, you would come up with a potentially endless list of subjective perspectives. However, I am going to keep it simple. For the sake of understanding the first of five dimensions, I will use the two interchangeably. My objective is not to distinguish between your conscious and your subconscious states of mind or what you dream about when you are fast asleep versus what you envision when you are awake. Rather, my objective is to awaken that deep-in-your-core foresight of impending greatness.

///

God-size visions and dreams have little to do with the end goal, although that matters, but everything to do with the transformative journey on your way to the goal.

///////

Put another way, a God-size vision or a God-size dream is often seen as a metaphor for an exceptionally ambitious goal that transcends our individual capacity and limitations. It represents a challenge that requires not just effort, but faith, hope, resilience, and a belief in something greater than us. God-size visions and dreams have little to do with the end goal, although that matters, but everything to do with the transformative journey on your way to the goal. These immensely grand dreams and visions inspire us to elevate our sight and push the boundaries of possibility, reminding us that remarkable potential to achieve greatness on a divine scale dwells within us all.

VIP PROTAGONISTS

Throughout this book, I will introduce two characters—our *Very Important Person* protagonists—who exemplify or embody the inevitable cycles that unfold across each of the five dimensions. These real-life protagonists, whether interpreted via a modern-day lens or viewed via their historical significance, help undergird dreams and visions with a sense of unwavering faith, resilience, and patient endurance. Like actors in a movie who, without warning, subliminally draw us into an experience that causes us to relate to their character, these protagonists remind us that even the loftiest of aspirations can materialize when entrusted to divine guidance and shaped through life's trials. Truth be told, I venture to take it a step further beyond our molding at the hands of the trials of life; I say that the fulfillment of these dreams and visions *will not* see the light of day without trying, difficult, and often chaotic moments in life.

Has every dream in your life become a reality without a challenge? Has your vision for something greater become a reality without interruptions, pitfalls, or failures? What do you think would happen, then, with a dream or a vision so grand that it transcends your personal limited abilities? Life's pitfalls *can* thwart them *unless* you understand the resources necessary to see them become a reality.

For instance, imagine being seventy-five years old and relatively successful. Thus far, nothing about your life suggests that you have missed the mark, underachieved, or failed to attain success. Yet, without any warning, your life is catapulted into an encounter so powerful that you are drawn into a vision unlike anything you have ever experienced before. Every bit of success you have experienced thus far dwarfs in comparison to the vision you now have.

Such was the case with an all-too-familiar figure in Genesis, the first book in the Holy Scriptures. Genesis 12:1-4 (NIV) puts it this way:

> The LORD said to Abram, "Go from your country, your people and your father's household to the land I will show you.
>
> "I will make you into a great nation, and I will bless you; I will make your name great, and you will be a blessing. I will bless those who bless you, and whoever curses you I will curse; and all peoples on earth will be blessed through you."

This call—this tugging at the core of his soul—undoubtedly propelled Abram to realize there was something greater about to take place in his life; something that would exceed his wildest expectations. Something that would not only change his familial status but also the course of history for future generations.

What about you? Where do *you* find yourself? Like Abram, have you experienced your share of success? Have you lived a fruitful life? What has success looked like for you? How do you define it? Is it a checklist of accomplished dreams you tick off at a certain age, scanning it from top to bottom and, with pen in hand, marking each item—

Check . . . check . . . check . . . check?

Now what? What's next? How big was your dream? How big was your vision? Was it a God-size dream that required God-size intervention? Was it a God-size vision that required divine guidance because, without it, you would have abandoned it amid opposition?

History is filled with those whom I consider to be proverbial VIP figures. Abram isn't the only person on the VIP list. Let me present to you another VIP who certainly epitomizes the fifth-dimension model.

Imagine you are a teenager, a seventeen-year-old young man. You lie down to sleep after a full day of chores and familial responsibilities. Nothing about this evening screams extraordinary. Then, one night, as you are sound asleep, you have a dream. Considering the agricultural environment you have grown accustomed to, a dream about sheaves in the field is nothing out of the ordinary. That is until the sheaves you bind remain upright while the sheaves the rest of your family bind bow down to yours (Genesis 37).

This teenager's name is Joseph. Like any young man working through levels of maturity and wisdom, he precipitously shares the dream with his brothers who immediately interpret it as arrogance. "Do you mean to reign over us? Do you mean to rule over us?" (Genesis 37:8, author paraphrase), his brothers suggested. Yet, before the effect of the first dream could dissipate, Joseph dreams another dream. This time, Joseph admits to his brothers, "The sun and moon and eleven stars were bowing down to me" (Genesis 37:9, NIV).

I could imagine that his father's berating response and his brothers' anger were not what he had anticipated. Yet, there he was, receiving backlash from his family for a dream he had not asked for and certainly one he could not fully understand. As if that were not enough, the disappointments, betrayal, loneliness, and heartache that cascaded from those dreams yet to materialize became the norm rather than the exception throughout Joseph's life. Instead of a promising road to the fulfillment of a dream, he experienced a personal journey that seemed to deviate entirely from it. As a matter of fact, his life became the antithesis of what progression should look like in the presence of a grand dream.

Can you relate? Do you have dreams that have been misunderstood, undervalued, or even buried under layers of impossibility, failure, or betrayal? Dreams so big, visions so grand, they scare you? As a matter of fact, nothing within your current economic status, familial pedigree, accomplishments, or bandwidth suggests that you have the full capacity to independently execute the fulfillment of that dream or see such a grand vision to completion. Does that scare you? Does it catapult you to push through unfamiliar territory or compel you to dawdle for fear of failure?

> **This book is about God-size dreams. It's about God-size visions. It is about dreams and visions that exceed your personal limitations.**

History is full of biblical heroes, heroines, and historical world changers who have transcended personal limitations to accomplish dreams and visions in ways that model ultimate resilience. However, I cannot say that without offering a point of clarification: this book is not about overcoming personal limitations to accomplish a personal dream or fulfill a personal vision. It is not the proverbial self-help manual that will motivate you to overcome obstacles, remain positive, and obtain levels of victory that will make you proud for not giving up.

Don't misunderstand me; there is nothing inherently wrong with any of those things. In a world with so many distractions and so much instability and cultural decadence, it takes a great deal of focus and resilience to overcome obstacles. It takes tenacity to fulfill dreams and experience the realization of a personal vision for success. Yet, this book is much more than that. This book is about God-size dreams. It's about God-size visions. It is about dreams and visions that exceed your personal limitations.

This framework encompasses a vast spectrum of people, transcending socioeconomic status, academic bandwidth, familial pedigree, or religious background. For instance, for Abram, one of our protagonists who will take center stage throughout the five dimensions, the vision embedded within him transcended economic success. He had already experienced earthly success with personal possessions. The vision was not something he could buy, grow, harvest, or manipulate into existence. It was too great for him to fully execute on his own. The same is true for Joseph. His young age would preclude him from the maturity and wisdom necessary to fuel a step-by-step progression toward the fulfillment of his dreams. But oh, no! His dreams were bigger and greater than anything he could individually formulate.

So, when I speak of heroes, heroines, and world-changers, I speak of people who overcame limitations, like those found in three of the five dimensions delineated throughout this book. Yet, despite those limitations, they consequently left a mark that changed history forever.

You may read this book and relate to the grand aspirations of someone who has made such an indelible mark on this world. Your dreams and visions are grand, yet you would admit they are greater than your personal limitations allow. Nonetheless, I encourage you to read on if you can envision an end in sight or would like to understand how the four dimensions on the way to fulfillment can either detain your dreams and visions from becoming a reality *or* propel them forward.

Conversely, maybe you were tempted to stop reading because you have sold yourself short. You could not relate to this idea of a hero, a heroine, or a world-changer who could produce such greatness that it would change your life and the lives of others. If that is you, then you have all the more reason to continue reading! Perhaps you cannot relate to a person like Abram who had already experienced success. But can you relate to a seventeen-year-old teenager with no prior experience in dream-building, let alone fueling such a grand dream until it became a reality? I can!

I FIT THE MODEL

I remember a television commercial in the late 1900s promoting hair restoration for men. After a lengthy pitch selling his product and hair-restoration system, the spokesperson ends the commercial by showing a picture of himself and exclaiming, "I am not only the hair club president, but I am also a client!" Well, I, too, cannot speak from a place I have not been. As such, I am not only the author, but I am also a living example of someone who has had to navigate the dimensions I outline in this book. How does a person with no academic model in his immediate or extended family, one who was bullied all throughout the course of elementary and middle school and, in many ways, was religiously shielded from the outside world, grow up to dream God-size dreams? How does that individual receive a vision for the future so deeply embedded in his soul that quitting is not an option? Well, I am that individual! Even as I pen this manuscript, I am reminded of one of my favorite texts in the Bible that has helped to sustain me through some of my most difficult moments: "*I would have despaired* unless I had believed that I would see the goodness of the LORD in the land of the living" (Psalm 27:13, NASB 1995, emphasis added). The potential for this desperation started early in my life. Let me give you a glimpse.

This is what I mean when I say I was religiously shielded from the outside world: though I am a Christian, I must admit that both my theology and praxis have come a long way from some of the teachings I was exposed to. I grew up in a religious environment that believed in the "the church should remain neutral" rule of thumb. This church neutrality meant engaging in church business (i.e., Sunday services, mid-week services, door-to-door sharing of our faith, youth groups, and anything else that simply engaged the "church" in fulfilling its mission) but nothing further. There was no such thing as the church engaging in politics, school programs, city sports programs, and the like. There seems to have been an unspoken theology that to engage in those areas was to mix with the world in an unhealthy and unspiritual way. Even at a young age, this didn't seem right to me.

For instance, as a young boy, I vividly remember standing on the grounds of one of the city's parks and grabbing onto a chain-linked fence. My nose poking in through one of the openings, I would watch the opening tryouts for the city's Little League baseball teams. I wanted so badly to try out for the team. However, my parents said no.

"Why?" I would argue.

"You know why," came their response with no hesitation, followed by something like, "The church programs and Sunday services will be in constant conflict with your practice and game days."

Part of me would get angry, and another part of me couldn't understand why people called to be light (Matthew 5:14-16) would be so adamantly segregated from the world around them.

So, was I limited to dreaming within the context of a church environment? If so, how would that impact the world around me? Was Joseph's dream, and ultimately, its fulfillment, simply geared toward a people linked to his heritage? How about your dreams? Are they limited to your upbringing? Is your vision contextualized within the limitations of your past experiences? Is your dream or vision restricted by failures, setbacks, betrayals, or boundaries those who preceded you have modeled? Well, like Joseph, it is time to dream again! Like Abram, it is time to come out of your comfort zone and believe that if you have been prompted by a vision greater than you, you are not to dismiss it as too grand, too lofty, or too impossible! Instead, you must ask yourself the question, *How will this dream or this vision become a reality?*

2

COME OUT! COME OUT WHEREVER YOU ARE!

*"You will never come out of your place of conformity
until you envision a better place!"*

"Conformity is the jailer of freedom and the enemy of growth."
—John F. Kennedy

I thought it was a figment of my imagination. Was my memory playing tricks on me, or was I taught to dream beyond my current condition at the young age of eight? I am now an adult dreaming grand dreams of my own. As if trying to dig for memories that would align with this stage in my life, this long-lost memory surfaced out of my memory bank. Was I imagining things? Because I wasn't certain, I picked up the phone and called my oldest sister. With a tone of confusion in my voice, I asked, "Nancy, did our cousin

Mayra . . ." (who, now that I think about it, was barely a teenager herself), "ask us to think and dream about big houses, beautiful furniture, and lavish vacations and promise to buy them for us when we grew older?"

"Oh, boy, did she," was her response. "Please tell me you remember the tan-colored composition notebook and orange marker she would always bring to capture our dreams on paper," she continued.

What would prompt a fourteen- or fifteen-year-old babysitter to dream beyond her limitations and engage others in the process? Maybe she, too, was a dreamer of God-size dreams. Truth is that she would travel periodically from her significantly run-down neighborhood in Philadelphia to a small apartment almost two hours away to babysit a couple of school-age children and prompt them to envision something far greater than their current environment. I don't know for sure what prompted such vivid imagination in this young lady's mind. One thing I do know is that my cousin Mayra's consistent ability to lift our minds out of the mundane— the comfortable and predictable—instilled a vision in me I still cherish to this day.

As I reminisce on those precious innocent memories of a child who did not fully understand the difference between fiction and reality, I am grateful that what may have been a ploy to keep a couple of seven- and eight-year-old children busy in a pre-digital culture turned out to become a catalyst for dreaming beyond the norm.

We were not the first and will not be the last prompted to dream outside of our current reality. Do you remember our biblical VIP protagonist, Abram? I wonder if that is what he felt like when he was promised a reward from God after his long drawn-out battle to rescue his nephew Lot from enemies (Genesis 14). Apparently, not realizing that God Himself was his reward, Abram retorted with an incredulous, "What good are all your blessings when I don't even have a son?" (Genesis 15:2, NLT) Scripture tells us that "the LORD took Abram outside and said to him, 'Look up into the sky and count the stars if you can. That's how many descendants you will have!'" (Genesis 15:5, NLT)

I can't seem to shake that phrase out of my head: "The Lord took Abram outside...." Abram was taken out of his dwelling place, out of his comfort zone, and out of his place of security, and asked to dream! The Lord's instructions to Abram meant that he would have to envision something beyond his limitations.

As he gazed at the vast expanse of the heavens above, the canopy of stars stretched out before him. In this moment of quiet contemplation, Abram found himself confronted not only with the majesty of the cosmos but also with the enormity of the dreams that stirred within his soul. He had to look beyond what he did not have and trust that something greater had been promised! Something so big that it transcended the wealth he had accumulated. For Abram, coming out of his tent to behold the stars was more than a simple act of stargazing—it was a profound encounter with the *Lord*. It was a stirring of the soul to dream God-size dreams. At this juncture, Abram had found inspiration to envision a future that transcended the boundaries of the present, a future where the promises of God are made manifest in the world around him. As he stood beneath the vast expanse of the heavens, Abram dared to imagine a legacy that would endure for generations to come, a legacy built not on earthly riches or fleeting pleasures but on faith, courage, and unwavering determination.

////////////////////////////////////

When your personal limitations end, God's unlimited possibilities begin.

//////////

Unlike Abram, who was successful and whose continual movement was made evident by his accomplishments, I was quite the opposite. Raised in a religious environment in which both parents fit the proverbial creatures-of-habit modus operandi, I could have easily acquiesced to every limitation possible. Please don't get me wrong. I had very loving, God-fearing parents who were married for fifty-one years until my mother passed from this earth at the early age of sixty-nine. Yet, they were creatures of habit who had conformed to the status quo. Our life was predictable. Day in and day out, month after month, and year after year, life did not change much. Life was not bad, but it was static. As such, I realized early on that it was difficult to come out of a place of conformity and complacency unless I envisioned a greater place.

What is *your* comfort zone? What have you been able to accomplish that you may feel has become your ceiling—the best you can give? Can I suggest that when your personal limitations end, God's unlimited possibilities begin? Abram's example teaches us that true greatness lies not in complacency but in the willingness to step beyond the confines of our comfort zones and into the realm of possibility. It is a reminder that to achieve God-size dreams, we must be willing to step out of familiar territory to embrace discomfort and trust in a higher purpose beyond our own understanding.

SCARED INTO ACTION

Embracing something beyond personal limitations is all too familiar to me. I still remember the call. As I sat with my hands tucked underneath my thighs, rocking back and forth and contemplating what I had just committed to, I thought, *Now what?* The president of a national organization had just called me and asked me to travel to our nation's capital and participate in a four-person panel in one of the Senate chambers on the topic of immigration reform. Initially, I thought, *No big deal.* I will make certain to have a team collaborate with me on the presentation and succinctly practice every detail. That is, until I found out who would be on the panel. Every panelist had a post-graduate degree. I didn't! As a matter of fact, other than formal theological education at an institute level, I didn't have a degree at all. What was I thinking? In a sense, I felt like Abram. I had experienced a certain level of success in banking management and was now following a tugging from God into pastoral ministry. Yet, academia, and more so, in the political realm, was not part of my resume . . . far from it!

As if the insecurities were not enough, a call from our city's mayor did not make it any better. He called the day before the presentation to tell me that he had learned I would be presenting in Washington, DC. He was already going to be in town for a mayor's meeting, so he intended to attend the event and listen to my presentation. At that point, I went from rehearsing my presentation to conjuring up multiple ways I could excuse myself from participating. Yet, amid all the conundrum, like Abram, I felt a tugging! A tugging with a voice. An internal voice that resounded within me, *Come out of your comfort zone and think bigger! You would not have received the invitation had someone not thought you capable of sitting at that table!*

How many of us are often tempted to pass on opportunities—God-size opportunities—because we do not feel qualified? Because we do not have the right degree, the right pedigree, the right socio-economic status, or the right experience? As such, it becomes easier to acquiesce to comfort—to conformity and complacency—than it is to charter unfamiliar territory. But what if that discomfort is precisely the preparation you need to catapult you into a dimension you had not considered? It did for me.

I spent a great deal of the twenty-four hours leading into the presentation in front of a mirror. I practiced hand placement, eye contact, verbal pauses, and inflection. I practiced, practiced, practiced. I prayed, and then I practiced some more. Finally, the hour came for me to walk into a room full of people, including politicians, representatives from multiple media outlets, and a moderator ready to ask questions.

I wish I could say that I remember most of the details from my experience in that environment. I don't! What I most remember was seeing the academic titles at the end of each of the presenters' nameplates and asking myself, *Why not me?* For as long as I can remember, I loved spending time with people who spoke well, people who were smarter than me and sharpened my skills. But considering the limitations that had surrounded me—albeit not by choice—I had dreamed only to the extent of my current reality. That was until I was pulled out of my place of conformity and dared to dream. At that moment I knew that because the dream was greater than my limitations, it would take God-size intervention to make a way for me to complete my graduate studies and ultimately earn my PhD. Please do not misconstrue my message (and here is a spoiler alert). Like Abram, who experienced the birth of a son by the name of Isaac, the PhD was not the fulfillment of a dream; it was only a taste of the God-size opportunities that would derive from stepping out of comfort into unchartered territory.

By the way, in case you are wondering, the panel turned out great. Like many of us, the worst-case scenarios I played out in my head did not materialize. No spilled cups of water from waving my hand too quickly. No fumbling words. No phrases or comments that did not align with the topic at hand. All that worry for nothing. Instead, any concern I had leading to this unfamiliar environment only made me better. Sound familiar?

True courage is not the absence of fear; rather, it is the willingness to confront and transcend it in pursuit of something greater.

A DIFFERENT PERSPECTIVE

It is time to view fear not as a deterrent but as a catalyst to change. Again, you will not come out of your place of conformity until you envision a better place. Like me, maybe you will be the first to attain a formal education. Or maybe you *were* the first in your family to attain a formal education. Like Abram, perhaps you have experienced unprecedented success, yet somehow you sense that it does not end there. You sense a stirring deep inside, prompting you to dream God-size dreams. At this point, you are tempted to match those dreams to the magnitude of your resources only to realize that they don't match. Great! Because God-size dreams require God-size resources.

The truth is that in this unveiling of life we call human existence, the comfort of familiarity often becomes a cozy cocoon, shielding us from the challenges and uncertainties that lie beyond its confines. Yet, it is in the daring act of stepping out of this place of comfort and conformity that we discover the true depths of our potential and our capacity to dream God-size dreams. Fear, like a relentless shadow, looms over our aspirations, whispering doubts and insecurities into our human-induced mental limitations. Fear becomes our adversary, seeking to immobilize us with its paralyzing grip and keep us tethered to the safety of the familiar. But true courage is not the absence of fear; rather, it is the willingness to confront and transcend it in pursuit of something greater.

In the face of fear and setbacks, daring to dream God-size dreams requires a resolute determination to press forward despite the odds. It is a journey fraught with obstacles and detours, yet it is precisely in overcoming these challenges that our faith is strengthened and our dreams are made manifest. Like Abram, are you ready? Are you ready to come out of your comfort zone, shift your eyesight from the natural to the supernatural, and dream God-size dreams?

In the end, it is not the absence of fear or setbacks that defines us but our willingness to rise above them and dare to dream with the audacity of those who believe in the limitless power of God. As we step boldly into the unknown, guided by faith and fueled by purpose, we unlock the boundless potential that lies within us and discover that the greatest adventures await those who dare to dream God-size dreams.

3

UNEXPECTED DREAMS

"Unexpected dreams often emerge from places of brokenness!"
—C. Olmeda

*"You have to take risks. We will only understand the miracle
of life fully when we allow the unexpected to happen."*
—Paulo Coelho

Dreams—God-size dreams—are birthed with purpose! Visions—God-size visions—are birthed with purpose. They are not given to you so that they may die with you when you take your last breath. They create changes that alter the course of life as we know it; changes that catapult families into experiencing a life their predecessors never experienced. They help to create habits, behaviors, and patterns that instill the idea that complacency is not an option.

The kind of dreams I refer to do not compare to the mundane musings of our daily lives. I am talking about the kind of dreams that defy logic. The ones that creep in through the crevices of a normal day. But when they trigger an unexpected emotion within the depth of your soul, you immediately realize that something is about to change. Take, for instance, the story of Nehemiah, a man—a biblical figure—whose life was forever altered by an unexpected dream. His journey from cupbearer to city builder holds timeless lessons for those who dare to hear the quiet whispers of unexpected dreams ready to invade an otherwise normal life.

Maybe Nehemiah's life was far from normal. I can imagine that living in a palace, serving a king, and adhering to protocols designed to meet the highest degree of excellence were not simple tasks. But when a desire to address a city-wide concern triggers an emotion within the crevices of his soul, he is catapulted to a new dimension of vision that transcends anything he has ever been accustomed to. So, why concede? Why take ownership of something he could have turned away from and walked in the opposite direction? I think the answer is complex—yet simultaneously simple. Complex, because to respond to such a prompting was to set off a series of events so grand that divine intervention would be needed. Simple, because it mattered. People's lives mattered. The condition of those he had an affinity for mattered. It mattered because something needed fixing, and he was the one prompted to action.

When similar things happen in our lives, we realize that sometimes, unexpected dreams are birthed out of necessity. The challenge lies in that we are not often privy to some of the changes considered necessary outside of our place of comfort until we are exposed to them. Further, we are not often exposed to much-needed changes until we come out of our place of complacency.

Before I delve into Nehemiah's timeless application, look at the unexpected prompting that changed the course of Jonathan's life (his name has been changed for anonymity). Jonathan accepted an open invitation I made to a group of men to join me on a speaking-engagement trip overseas. Now, I must be completely transparent here. The truth is, when I travel for speaking engagements, I am not one for "high-maintenance relationships." I don't want to look after those who travel with me or deal with any sort of drama that often arises when groups travel together. I can hear it already: "Someone's luggage is too heavy" or "Someone just got delayed going through the airport security checkpoint." I don't do well with those sorts of circumstances. (Please don't judge me; God is still working with me.) Instead, I am focused on the task before me, the people I will be speaking to, and the message I am about to deliver. Nonetheless, I chose to open this event to whoever wanted to attend.

Jonathan, along with four other men and me, arrived at the airport in what seemed like a trouble-free trip. That is until I noticed that Jonathan was watching every single move I made. If I didn't know any better, I would have said that he thought he was my personal bodyguard (I don't have a bodyguard, by the way). So, guess what I am thinking? You're right! I am thinking, *Here we go! This is beginning to turn into some weird, high-maintenance relationship!* Regardless, I ignored my personal assessment of him and went about my business trying to ignore Jonathan's proximity and mimicking behavior. This went on all the way to our destination, at which point I was grateful we would not be roommates.

All throughout the trip, the group of men traveling with me and I engaged in all sorts of conversations. Topics ranged from sports to spirituality, family life, work life, and, interestingly enough, God-size dreams. During one of our conversations, I remember sharing stories about the changes that had taken place in my life, ultimately leading me to accomplish many things and build my family in ways I never had before. Through it all, I noticed a blank stare from Jonathan.

I was due to speak the night of our arrival, leaving us with free time throughout the next day before having to speak again that night. During our free time, one of my staff members and I stopped by Jonathan's room to invite him and some of the other men for a game of basketball. Although basketball is not my forte, I thought that some much-needed exercise beneath the island sun would do us good. A couple of the guys invited us in as they gathered their belongings. In an unexpected turn of events, Jonathan said, "Hey, Pastor Charles, can I share something with you?" Before I could answer, he said, "I need to apologize."

"What do you need to apologize for?" I asked.

"I need to apologize for my behavior," he quickly responded. And without hesitation, he started describing the very behavior I had been concerned about since arriving at the airport. He spoke about his proximity to me, the mimicking of my every move, and his quiet stares while I shared my personal stories. Suddenly, without forewarning, with tears running down his cheeks, he said, "I know without a doubt I had to accompany you on this trip!"

Awkwardly, I was thinking, *Where is this going?*

As he tried to regain his composure, he said, "This is my first time traveling like this. I have never flown before. So, I asked myself, how do I follow in his footsteps without asking so many questions or disturbing his focus? So, I decided to do whatever you did."

Fine, I am thinking, *but why are you crying?!*

As if he could hear my thoughts, he went ahead to explain how although he was a grown man, married for thirteen years with a solid career, he couldn't help but look at me as a father figure. As such, he had spent the last day and a half pondering my stories. So much so, that he started to dream about what would happen if he emulated some of the things that God had used to pull *me* out of *my* own conformity and complacency.

"I have been married for thirteen years, and I have never taken my family on a vacation," he admitted. "I have been a creature of habit, living in complacency and afraid to dream God-size dreams," he went on to admit. "But as I hear you speak, something has come alive in me! When I go back home, I must make some changes that will change the course of my future generations," he sternly suggested. And that he did.

A month later, Jonathan surprised his family with a dream vacation they had never experienced before. He went on to dream God-size dreams and expand his bandwidth by buying investment properties, helping his wife become an entrepreneur, and changing the trajectory of his future generations.

When I think about Jonathan, I can't help but think that, quite often, the kinds of dreams that pull us out of complacency are birthed out of brokenness. For Jonathan, his newfound dreams were birthed out of generational challenges too extensive to articulate in this story.

In an instant, like Nehemiah, Jonathan was prompted into action from hearing ONE story—but one with consequences reaching far outside of himself. If he didn't answer the call to that conviction, his family would pay for his inaction. He leaped into action, came out of his place of comfort and complacency, and emulated changes that would forever change the course of future generations.

///

Dreams without action can become nightmares.

///////

Can you picture it? One moment, Nehemiah is serving within the comfort of a palace, and the next moment, he is organizing the funding process and construction of city walls. Why? Because he heard a story. A story of people who had endured oppression and had been released by their captors but were living amongst ruins back in their homeland. Can you imagine that? You aren't living in captivity (you are "free") but still live amid ruins until someone else's comfort is shaken by a God-size dream that will change the course of your life forever. However, dreams alone don't transform reality. Unexpected dreams demand resilience. Nehemiah knew that he had to meticulously plan, mobilize resources, and rally people if those dreams were going to become a reality. He knew that dreams without action can become nightmares.

How about you? What places of comfort and complacency is God wanting to pull you out of to give you dreams that will change the course of your life forever? Don't minimize Jonathan's dreams because they were personal, familial, and practical. No! They serve as a reminder that the course of future generations can be transformed because people like you and I decide to be fully present and listen to the unfamiliar sound of dreams and visions resounding in the atmosphere that seek to permeate our soul and prompt us to make changes. They prompt us to dream bigger and envision a life much more rewarding than our status quo. Our children do not have to settle for our complacency. Our future generations don't have to inherit our mistakes, our falters, or our failures. Instead, they can become recipients of new beginnings that do not compare to the challenges we may have endured.

> **Our children do not have to settle for our complacency.**

For Nehemiah, the walls he set out to build were completed in fifty-two days. He faced fatigue, doubt, and fear. Yet, he pressed on. Jerusalem stood tall once more—a testament to unwavering faith and relentless effort. So, please let me remind you, your unexpected dreams await. Whether you're rebuilding walls or rewriting stories, remember Nehemiah's legacy. Embrace the unexpected, for therein lies your destiny.

4

MISUNDERSTOOD

"Being misunderstood is often part of the process!"
—C. Olmeda

*"Never waste your time explaining who you are to people
who are committed to misunderstanding you."*
—Author Unknown

Dreams that are larger than life—God size dreams—often
come with a vision that transcends the ordinary and challenges the status quo. These are the dreams that speak of change,
of doing something significant, of impacting the world in ways that
most people can't even fathom. But with such grand dreams comes
the inevitable reality of being misunderstood.

Misunderstanding is a common thread in human interactions,
often leading to conflict and estrangement. It can stem from differences in communication, perception, or simply the unique way
individuals process and share their inner thoughts and visions. The

story of Joseph is a profound example of how being misunderstood can lead to dire consequences, yet also pave the way for redemption and greater purpose.

In this same vein, jealousy is a complex emotion that arises when someone else's success or aspirations threaten our own sense of self-worth or position. When you present a dream that is vast and seemingly unattainable, it can make others feel small or inadequate, leading to jealousy. They may not grasp the depth of your vision or the faith that fuels it, and in their misunderstanding, they may respond with skepticism or even hostility.

TIME IS YOUR BEST FRIEND

I will never forget sitting in my office as one of my lead staff members knocked on the door. Before I could say, "Come in," he barged in and, without hesitation, demanded, "You have to do something!" By the concerned look on his face, whatever he was referring to seemed quite serious.

"What in God's name are you talking about?" I quickly responded.

He retorted, "Your character and integrity are at risk of being tarnished if you don't respond to the accusations." Truthfully, I had no idea what he was talking about until I helped him calm down to explain.

At the time, along with my wife, I was a fairly new pastor of a small congregation that had outgrown a shared space with another congregation in a different town. By divine providence and via the tireless pursuit of a wife whose resilience and faith led to the acquisition of a building thirty times bigger than the space we were renting, we were now in a space we could call our own in the next town over.

Unbeknownst to me, a leader from a nearby church had started to spread rumors about why our church was rapidly growing. Rumors that, in hindsight, were grotesque. It was difficult to understand how anyone would believe such embellishment, let alone about two individuals this leader had never met. I cannot attest to his rumors being part of a larger conspiracy—to the credit of his congregation. Yet, here we were. Like someone cutting open a feather pillow at the top of a mountain on a windy day, his rumors had flown far and wide and were now difficult to collect.

As the staff member instigated me to do something, I quickly responded, as if prompted by divine direction, "Stop! Leave it alone! Time is our best friend!"

"But Pastor—" he continued.

"Please, trust me. Leave it alone! Time is our best friend!" I said.

By the look on his face, I knew he thought my decision was wrong. Yet, he dropped the subject and walked away.

About three months later, a group of thirteen or fourteen leaders, including me and the leader who had barged into my office, walked into a restaurant not too far from our new property. As we were seated, whom did I spot across the room? None other than the leader from the nearby church who had spread baseless rumors about me, my wife, and our congregation. As soon as we were seated, I saw him get up from his table and make his way to where we were seated. I was seated at the head of the table, and to my right was the staff member who had wanted me to address the rumors. The leader from the other church, without asking any permission whatsoever, proceeded to approach our table, walked up to where I was seated, and bent one knee as if to say something to my staff member and me.

A resentful heart full of bitterness and unforgiveness affects us more than it does the offender. As he knelt, I thought, *This guy has nerves of steel! Maybe I should have heeded my staff member's insistence and said something while I had a chance.*

Yet, as one thought after another raced through my head, the man leaned in and said, "Please forgive me for interrupting your dinner, but when I saw you come in, I could not let another minute go by without coming over to apologize!" He proceeded to share how he had spoken on matters that he did not understand and allowed his fear of competition to bring out the worst in him . . . so much so that he almost sabotaged his own ministry! I could sense a genuine, remorseful, repentant heart as he apologized. Without hesitation, I accepted his apology, stood up from my seat, shook his hand, and off he went.

As I sat down, my staff member looked at me and said, "Thank God you didn't fight that battle. Time was indeed our best friend!"

Forgiveness is key to moving forward. A resentful heart full of bitterness and unforgiveness affects us more than it does the offender. It has the tendency to place on our shoulders unnecessary, emotional weight that slows down our progress. Someone once said that unforgiveness is like choosing to stay trapped in a jail cell of bitterness and serve time for someone else's crime. Forgive! It will allow you to move forward and see the fulfillment of God-size dreams.

As the leader from the other church walked away, I wondered if he understood that as we moved into that nearby location, like Joseph, our dreams were not just personal aspirations; they were revelations of a future that God had ordained. For Joseph, his brothers—unable to understand or accept the divine origin and significance of his dreams—allowed their jealousy to guide their actions, leading to Joseph's betrayal and suffering. To them, Joseph's visions were a threat to their own standing within the family, a sign of arrogance, or simply fantasies of a favored younger sibling.

IT DOESN'T END THIS WAY

Please understand that being misunderstood does not define your worth or your future. It shows that even when you are misjudged, maligned, or mistreated, there is a greater plan at work, one that uses your unique gifts and circumstances to bring about a greater good. It's a reminder that the path to fulfilling your destiny can be fraught with trials but also that perseverance and faith can lead to unexpected and triumphant outcomes.

Joseph's story didn't end in despair. Neither did ours. Despite being misunderstood and mistreated, Joseph remained steadfast to his God-given dreams. Joseph's unwavering faith and perseverance eventually led to a position of power and influence that not only proved his detractors wrong but also enabled him to save countless lives during a time of famine.

Remaining steadfast to your dreams, especially when they are misunderstood, is a testament to your faith and conviction. It's about holding on to what you believe is your calling despite the doubts and negativity that may come from others. It's about understanding that the fulfillment of such dreams often requires a journey through hardship and adversity, which serves to prepare and strengthen you for the role you are meant to play.

Like Joseph, you may encounter situations where you feel misunderstood. You may face ridicule, isolation, or betrayal because others cannot grasp your vision or intentions. Allow Joseph's journey to encourage you to hold fast to your dreams and to trust that, in time, their purpose will be revealed, not only to you but also to those who once doubted you. It's a call to remain steadfast in the face of misunderstanding that is often the crucible in which your character is tested, and your ultimate purpose is forged.

> ## God-size dreams will always be met with a degree of misunderstanding and jealousy.

When you stay true to your God-size dreams, you embody the resilience and determination that are necessary to bring them to fruition. You become living proof that dreams, no matter how big, are achievable. Your success then becomes a beacon of hope and inspiration for others, showing them that what may seem impossible is merely a challenge waiting to be overcome.

In pursuing your dreams, you also set an example of grace and forgiveness. Just as Joseph forgave his brothers, understanding that their actions were part of a larger plan, you too, can rise above the pettiness of jealousy and offer compassion. This not only heals old wounds but also paves the way for others to join you in your vision, transforming skeptics into allies.

God-size dreams will always be met with a degree of misunderstanding and jealousy. It's a natural response to something that challenges the norm. But by staying steadfast in your pursuit, you validate the worth of your dreams. You prove that with faith, perseverance, and a heart willing to forgive, what others see as folly can indeed become a reality that benefits many. Your journey then becomes a powerful narrative of triumph over adversity, a story that will encourage others to dare to dream just as big.

Beware: choosing to move forward with a God-size dream and a God-size vision is risky business. Don't expect to experience such a grand fulfillment of dreams and visions that transcend the status quo without some bumps, twists, and turns along the way.

5

TIME IS YOUR BEST FRIEND

"It is not 'if' your dreams will be fulfilled, but 'when!'"
—C. Olmeda

*"The most important lesson I learned is that first you have
to dream, and then you have to believe in your dreams.
That is the only way for them to come true."*
—Caroll E. Spinney

Throughout the last few chapters, you have navigated through the exhilarating possibility of an emerging dream—a vivid vision of what lies ahead—like Abram; the vision is so grand that the multiplied outcome derived from what you produce cannot be numbered. The dream is so vivid that you visualize yourself standing in the majesty of its fullness. Yet, in what feels like the blink of an eye, you ask yourself, *Was this real? Was the dream a figment of my imagination?* Was the vision so grandiose that maybe—just maybe—you dreamed of having greater abilities than what you currently have, if only for a moment? So much so that even if your bandwidth increased, you would still be reaching for something unattainable? I find that these thoughts often surface when setbacks creep in and attempt to sabotage our dreams. When that happens, let me remind you that time is your best friend *or* your worst enemy! Time reveals all things!

Think about our protagonist Joseph. He wakes up, and before his feet can touch the ground, he is contemplating how quickly he can gather his brothers and share the magnitude of his dream with them. Yet, after two rounds of sharing what his brothers felt was some level of narcissistic rendering of a baseless dream, Joseph is now spiraling hopelessly into a pit. Perhaps Joseph was presumptuous in sharing his dream. Likewise, maybe his brothers should have considered their familial connection rather than allowing a dream yet to be fulfilled to threaten them. Either way, in a matter of moments, what was potentially an attainable dream now feels beyond reach. That is both the beauty and detriment of time. For all of us, time flows, sometimes gently and other times turbulently. In the process, your dreams face erosion—the slow wearing down of enthusiasm and battering setbacks. *Here* is where persistence becomes your ally.

> ## Obstacles aren't roadblocks; they're stepping stones.

Why persist? Because, like Abram, you have been created for something greater than what you have experienced via your own efforts. Like Joseph, you will mature into the person bearing all the qualities and qualifications necessary to play your role in the fulfillment of the dream. The architect of the dream life knows that progress isn't linear. It's the unwavering commitment to keep chiseling, keep building, keep writing, keep leaping—even when time seems against you.

For Joseph, time was relentless and impartial; it threw obstacles in his way. For many of us, health falters, relationships strain, and resources dwindle. Yet, the dreamer persists. We scale mountains of doubt, traverse valleys of fear, and bridge chasms of uncertainty. We learn that obstacles aren't roadblocks; they're stepping stones. They shape us and fortify our resolve.

BULLIED INTO DESTINY

You remember the aspiring dreamer in chapter two who drew houses, pictures of furniture, and lavish vacations, all because his babysitter enjoyed fueling dreams? Remember him? Yes, that was me! And I will admit that in the quiet corners of that eight-year-old boy's heart, dreams took root. Initially, they felt like fantasies, adventures that stretched beyond the schoolyard. As I grew, they became more realistic. But life, relentless and unyielding, had other plans.

Dreams turned into nightmares. As a school-age child with a unibrow and often dressed in dress pants with sneakers, what should have been a rush of freedom to peacefully leave the school building and enjoy life, became a race for my life. As far back as I can remember, I became the weak kid bullies picked on. My parents were not people to engage in any sort of confrontation. My dad was a bi-vocational minister *and* truck driver, and my mother was a stay-at-home mom. Between Dad's on-the-road responsibilities and his ministry duties the rest of the time, the only other person I had to depend on was my mother. Yet, with her gentle soul, soft-spoken, and extremely God-fearing demeanor, she never promoted violence or even self-defense. So, by default, I did the only thing I knew how to do . . . run!

Year after year, the bullies emerged—their taunts like thunderstorms, their jeers like penetrating daggers. The dreamer now becomes the object of their mockery! Even as I write, I am reminded of how overwhelming some of my actions were, like escaping to my only safe place—my home—and lying down to sleep every moment I had available. By today's psychotherapy classification, those actions may be labeled as depression. Maybe they were! I couldn't tell you for sure. But one thing I can tell you, I continued to dream God-size dreams. At the time, they may have been a form of escape. In hindsight, it was God's way of catapulting me to destiny.

///

As long as I had a dream, I would reach for the stars, even if I had to crawl through the mud first.

////////

In my solitude, I would often say, *One day. . . !* I would encourage myself that, one day, I would beat the daylights out of one of the bullies (that's a great story for a later time). The older I got, the more precise my declarations became. *One day, I will put them all to shame. One day, my success will speak for itself.* Years later, I would realize that God had gifted me with an understanding of the role that time plays. Throughout that time period, time was both my best friend and my worst enemy—my best friend because the pursuit of something greater than my current circumstance became the proverbial dangling carrot offering a glimpse of hope and my worst enemy because pain tends to obscure dreams. So, how do you navigate such parallels if not by relying on the Dream-Giver and persisting despite the adversity?

What crossroads have you encountered? What life bullies have attempted to shatter your dreams into nonexistence? As a leader to leaders and as a leader with a heart to mentor the next generation of world-changers, I cannot tell you how many stories I have heard of obstacles and setbacks. From personal and immoral failures to health challenges, from divorces and bankruptcies to the loss of loved ones, and from depression and anxiety to the desire to end it all—people have experienced unfathomable things that often obfuscate any sense of a God-size dream. Despite the challenges, don't stop now. Time is your best friend.

Dreams without action remain wisps of smoke. I had to act. YOU must act!

For me, I mastered the art of ignoring. The bullies' words became distant echoes. Each insult fueled my determination. As long as I had a dream, I would reach for the stars, even if I had to crawl through the mud first. As I ponder on my life, I realize that the bullies' punches could not bruise my imagination. My dreams—my visions—became my armor. As I understood the origin of my dreams, I further realized that I was covered with the armor of my Creator.

In a letter to the Ephesians, the apostle Paul admonished them to "put on all of God's armor so that [they would] be able to stand firm against all strategies of the devil" (Ephesians 6:11, NLT). As the armor shielded my life, the dreams became life. The boy became a man, and like clay in a potter's hands, the dreams took form. They were too grand to be bruised by senseless, insecure bullies who were probably seeking approval and status through a false sense of power. The more time passed, the clearer the dreams became.

The clearer the dreams, the more action was demanded of me. Slipping into a fetal position to escape my reality could not and would not offer a true escape. Dreams without action remain wisps of smoke. I had to act. YOU must act! Action is the catalyst to fulfillment. As the years passed, I acted. I enrolled in the choir, the vocal ensemble, and theology classes, and I received my emergency medical technician certification . . . all before the age of seventeen. The more I pressed on, the more opportunities presented themselves. One door led to another . . . that led to another . . . and to another. I quickly learned that as we act, unforeseen paths become visible, and resilience becomes the catalyst to momentum.

The bullies may scoff, but the fulfillment of the dream awaits in the distance, cheering you on.

Was that not the case with our protagonist, Joseph? One moment, time would surface as an enemy, attempting to dissipate the essence of his dreams. The next moment, time would arise with hope and wonder, causing his bullies' actions to serve as a catalyst to the next phase of his dreams. In either situation, time helped define his life. As time passed, Joseph realized that the dream life wasn't static. Like Joseph, we must come to the same realization. Time is our silent companion, navigating us through peaks and valleys, ultimately weaving our dreams into an intricately woven fabric of reality until we see its fulfillment—if we do not give up.

So, fellow dreamer, hold tight. The bullies may scoff, but the fulfillment of the dream awaits in the distance, cheering you on. Its fullness will become your legacy. Before you know it, God will set up a table in the presence of your enemies (Psalm 23:5). I have experienced this through the years. In a culture of global access, social media has become the microscope, amplifying the progress of many. As such, I have crossed paths with many of the students familiar with my journey, only for them to realize that instead of being bullied into despair, I was bullied into destiny.

2ND DIMENSION

FAILURE OR BETRAYAL

DREAMS
&
VISIONS

FAILURE
OR
BETRAYAL

6

WHEN FAILURE BECOMES PART OF THE PROCESS

"Success is not final; failure is not fatal. . . . It is the courage to continue that counts."
—Winston Churchill

Tick tock! Tick tock! Tick tock! The proverbial clock is ticking, and your dreams have become a distant memory. Not because you have intentionally forgotten them but because time has dragged them into oblivion. At this juncture, you begin to second-guess whether your dream was a God-size dream after all. Or perhaps that is exactly what it was—a God-size dream for which you were unprepared and ill-equipped. If you're like me, thoughts like, *Has God forgotten me?* or *How can this dream become a reality considering my current circumstance?* become the norm rather than the exception. It is at this crossroads that failure creeps in like a

71

slithering snake making its way through the crevices of doubt and despair. When it does, what will you do?

How can something that once felt so good now feel so bad? The transition between dimension one (dreams/visions) and dimension two (failure/betrayal) *will* come, so you should expect it! There is no easy way for me to say it. Expect it! However, you should also know that it is not where your dreams and visions end! There is more!

Remember our infamous protagonist, Abram? That's right, the one with a multi-generational promise so grand that even if he attempted to count his blessings, he would lose count time and time again. Yes, the man who was so advanced in age that producing a child should have been out of the question. And to complicate matters, his wife, too, was past childbearing age ... by decades, not years. So why did Sarai suggest to her husband Abram, "Go and sleep with my servant. Perhaps I can have children through her" (Genesis 16:2, NLT)? This seems like the obvious alternative to producing a child from her own body, considering her perceived inability to bear children.

I can parse the "Go sleep with my servant" suggestion over several pages in an attempt to make sense of Sarai's thought process. But I won't. My focus instead is the word *perhaps*: "Perhaps I can have children through her!" Why? Because many of us are like Sarai, are we not? We become impatient when we don't understand the timeline of the vision or the God-size dream embedded within us.

How many people have delayed the fulfillment of dreams— the realization of a vision—because they have taken matters into their own hands? Some have abandoned or aborted their dreams because the delay was too extensive. "My finances are not doing too well, so *perhaps* I can borrow money as an easy fix!" "My relationship is going through turmoil, so *perhaps* I can find someone else who will make me happy!" "My business is not as profitable as I think it should be, so *perhaps* I can take some shortcuts . . . cheat a little and lie a little. Who will ever know?" These questions and many like them become all-too-familiar suggestions when the fulfillment of a vision seems stagnant.

///

We must be careful because desperate measures often invoke unintended consequences.

////////

Like Abram, the weight of unfulfilled expectations often presses down on us, and doubt creeps in. When it does, the longing for a fulfilled dream—the realization of a vision—collides with impatience. In an instance, what was once a beacon of hope becomes a web of confusion. How many of us, like Abram, instead of waiting on God's timing, will seek to fulfill *the promise* in our own way? This act of attempting to manipulate a divine plan led to conflict and turmoil within Abram's household. Sarai grew resentful! Hagar, Sarai's servant, who has now given birth to Abram's child, faces mistreatment. Despite the temporary fulfillment of a desire for progeny, the consequences of this failure were profound.

Like Hagar, others can find themselves in a web of challenges because of premature decision-making. Ever heard the adage,

"Desperate times call for desperate measures?" Well, we must be careful because desperate measures often invoke unintended consequences. In the web of despair, we can drag spouses, children, friends, or coworkers into our mess and entangle them in the aftermath of choices they did not make. The spillover effect of our choices can have dire consequences.

Failure is not always a result of external circumstances or bad luck; sometimes, it stems from our own moral shortcomings. Unfortunately, I have experienced it several times in my life. Perhaps you have too. It takes an individual with a lack of a moral compass to not sense the debilitating weight of the aftermath of failure. Relationships have been severed because of personal failure. Marriages have ended in divorce because of personal failure. Businesses and ministries alike have dissolved because of personal failure.

Quite often, a loss of time, resources, and emotional instability ensue when failure invades our journey toward the fulfillment of a vision. When that happens, the heart-wrenching devastation can paralyze our efforts to keep moving forward. So, what will you do? Will you succumb to the painful realization that your God-given dream has been interrupted by none other than yourself? Will you succumb to the idea that the momentum to the fulfillment of your vision has lost its speed? Or will you dare acknowledge that the dream is too big—the vision too grand—for personal limitations to abort it? Remember, it was never about a dream that *you* could fulfill in your own effort anyway. It was never about a vision that could materialize by engaging *your* personal aptitude. The dream is bigger than your limited efforts. The vision is greater than your human limitations.

LESSONS FROM FAILURE

There is another factor to consider when you have succumbed to an action leading to failure. The question is not, "How devastating were the ramifications of my failures?" Spiraling down the painful memory lane of improprieties can have long-lasting emotional effects and keep you stagnant. So be careful with spending too much time soaking in sorrow. Why not learn from those failures and take an inventory of what needs to change so that those actions are not repeated? The painful sting of failure should be strong enough to remind you that the decision you made may not have been the right one but also create enough discomfort to make whatever changes necessary so that those actions are not repeated.

Trust me, I am not exempt from this live-and-learn growth process. One night, as I was working on my dissertation for my doctoral degree, I worked late into the night. After catching a second wind, I saw the sun come up as the bright rays of sunshine pierced through my window. As I contemplated the insanity of having worked through the night, I asked myself, *Is it worth it?* Adding to the melancholic sentiment was the thought of how I had made sacrifices by not spending time with friends and participating in activities that I knew I would thoroughly enjoy. Just as quickly as those thoughts inundated my mind, I was quickened by a distant memory of a missed opportunity that I came to regret.

Twenty-plus years prior to that moment, I was taking two years of Spanish and one year of French in high school. At the end of one of my Spanish classes, I was presented with an opportunity to meet with my Spanish teacher on a Saturday morning and take a test that would secure me a scholarship to Spain during that following summer. I was scheduled for the test when I received a call from a friend the night before inviting me to go away for the weekend and visit some friends in Upstate New York. His convincing rhetoric and list of reasons for how I would get other opportunities were enough to lure me into heeding such ridiculous and regretful behavior. How could I have passed on a semester in Spain for a weekend of senseless pleasure?

//

You either pay now and play later, or you play now and pay later, but sooner or later, you have to pay.

///////////

I returned to class the following week, and as the sting of a missed opportunity set in, I tried to find every justifiable reason to appease my conscience. None of it worked. I had failed to make the right decision, and I knew it. Now, I had to either live with regret or learn from my poor decision. I quickly learned that whatever you don't control will ultimately control you. I either had to learn to control my live-for-the-moment desires, or they would control me. I had to learn that in life, you either pay now and play later, or you play now and pay later—sooner or later, you have to pay. You have to pay with time, effort, resources, and sacrifices to remain focused and see your God-size dreams become a reality, or else you will waste your life *playing* and then pay the painful price of lost time and lost opportunities.

At that moment, I snapped out of my stupor of regret. As the rays of the sun beamed through my window, I had to remind myself,

Charles, you are familiar with the sting of failure. So, pay now and play later! When you get your degree, you will be able to bask in the reward of knowing that the past no longer serves as a weight of regret but as a catapult to better decisions and God-given opportunities.

I can rattle off a list of poor decisions, shortcomings, and blatant failures I have endured throughout my life. From financial and business decisions to poor time management and relational challenges, I will be the first to tell you that none of us is exempt from decisions we have come to regret. Yet, *I* had to decide. Do I spiral down the vortex of regret and repeat the same actions time and time again? Or do I allow my failures to serve as a catapult to new decision-making and practices that turn my failures into lessons?

One of the saddest things to see is people who have failed due to poor decisions and continue to repeat the same practices time and time again. They often engage in the same behaviors and, like the quintessential definition of insanity, continue to do the same thing over and over again while expecting different results. Have you been there? Do you find yourself on the proverbial hamster wheel of never-ending failure? I hate to be the bearer of bad news, but let me remind you that if nothing changes, then nothing changes. The sting of your past failures must produce a desire to change, to see yourself in a better place. Remember what I said about Abram in chapter 1? You will not come out of your place of complacency until you envision a better place.

When in doubt, remember that you are not alone in this personal journey of apparent setbacks. By no means am I making excuses for personal failure, nor am I suggesting you justify bad behavior, unethical decisions, questionable actions, or immorality. For many reasons too numerous to list here, we, as human beings living in a fallen world, tend to engage in actions that often derail us from a smooth journey toward the fulfillment of a God-size vision.

For instance, think about Richard Nixon, the thirty-seventh President of the United States, who experienced an ignominious downfall due to the Watergate scandal. His involvement in illegal activities tarnished the highest office in the land. However, Nixon's resilience came to the fore during his post-presidential years. He wrote books, engaged in diplomacy, and worked toward reconciliation. His ability to rebuild his reputation after such moral failure serves as a testament to human resilience.

How about Lance Armstrong, the celebrated cyclist who achieved unprecedented success but later admitted to doping throughout his career? His fall from grace was swift and severe. However, Armstrong's resilience lies in his post-scandal endeavors. He shifted focus to cancer advocacy, raising millions for research and support. Despite his moral failings, Armstrong's commitment to a greater cause showcases the power of redemption.

The list can go on and on. Steve Jobs, the cofounder of Apple, faced professional setbacks and made mistakes to the point of being ousted from his own company. However, Jobs returned with a renewed vision, ultimately revolutionizing technology and design. His resilience transformed him into an icon, reminding us that failure need not be the end of our story.

What about David, the "man after God's own heart" (1 Samuel 13:14; Acts 13:22)? Does it get any worse than that? Instead of focusing on the task at hand, David slid down the slippery slope of distraction and took a married woman into the hidden chambers of intimacy. As if that were not bad enough, he attempted to pin her unexpected pregnancy on her husband, who turned out to be more ethically and morally aligned than he was. When that shameful plan disintegrated, David directed that he be killed. One cannot negate that the devastation, pain, and long-term effects of his decision followed him for many years. Yet, through acknowledgment and repentance, he was able to fulfill God-size dreams.

Failure is not the end of your story unless you surrender to it.

It is at this point that I must draw your attention to this book's framework. I will do that repeatedly as a reminder that regardless of what dimension you find yourself in, you must look forward to the dimension that follows. No dimension, as set forth throughout this book, lasts forever. What does that mean for you? It means that failure is not the end of your story unless you surrender to it.

Unfortunately, I am familiar with numerous examples of people whose burden of pain, shame, and failure became so heavy that they succumbed to its devastating weight. Some chose to take their own lives. Others abandoned their dreams. Yet, others decided to coast through life merely surviving. I often wonder if they would have made the same decision if they understood what dimension was looming on the horizon. Would their outcome have been different had they understood that failure or its debilitating effects did not have to be the end of the story? What if we learned from those who came before us and refused to treat failure as a long-lasting open wound? Instead, they allowed time to heal its piercing effect and returned to the realization that their dream was bigger than their failure and their vision could become clearer than the obscurity of a mistake.

The individuals mentioned herein, and many others, teach us that moral failings and personal mistakes do not have to be permanent roadblocks. Resilience, self-reflection, and a commitment to growth can lead to redemption and triumph. As we navigate our lives, may their stories inspire us to rise above our imperfections and forge a path toward greatness.

7

WHEN BETRAYAL BECOMES PART OF THE PROCESS

"The saddest thing about betrayal is that it never comes from your enemies; it comes from those you trust the most."
—Author Unknown

What if failure isn't the only cause of stagnation—"Wait! It was not my fault!" you exclaim as you find yourself on the receiving end of betrayal. For many, possibly including you, it is not personal failure that has brought your dreams and vision to a screeching halt, but rather, unexpected challenges, like unprovoked betrayal! In many instances, betrayal is convoluted because it often does not come from people you have no vested interest in. No! It often comes from those closest to you!

Remember Joseph? This young man, favored by his father, had been gifted a coat of many colors. Between his colorful, resplendent appearance and his newly acquired dreams, his future looked promising! His destiny seemed irrevocably intertwined with greatness. Despite his pathway to success, Joseph had missed one thing, though not through personal choice. The betrayal of those closest to him had not been calculated into the equation toward the fulfillment of his dreams. His brothers, consumed by jealousy upon the interpretation of their young sibling's newly revealed dreams, conjured up one of the worst cases of betrayal anyone could imagine. Their disdain for Joseph shattered their familial trust, fractured their bonds, and plunged Joseph into what I can imagine was an abyss of emotional darkness.

For you and me alike, betrayal becomes a journey we never willingly embark on, yet life thrusts it upon us and leaves us standing at the crossroads between a feeling of what is and what could have been. It is at this crossroads of uncertainty that we must begin to acquiesce—albeit temporarily—to a path we did not choose. Like being caught in an unexpected mudslide, we must now ride this filthy and often bitter breach-of-trust journey while battling thoughts of how things could have turned out differently.

I can still feel the mood in the room and the pain in the voices of so many people who have come through my office and shared their feelings of betrayal. "I thought he loved me! How could he do this to me?" "I thought she loved me! How could she be with someone else?" "I trusted him!" "I trusted her!" "They were family members!" "How could they abuse me?" "We grew up together! How could she lie to me?" "I mentored him and gave him the position he has enjoyed! How could he turn his back on me as if I didn't play a role in his life?" The countless stories are different, but the sentiments are the same. A heart-piercing cry of confusion, often mixed with anger, and more questions than answers tend to fill the room. Truth be told, in those moments, there is very little you can do or say to make things better. Usually, the wounds are too fresh and the pain too deep for words of comfort to appease them. They help, but they don't take away the pain. Like our protagonist Joseph, we must wait for time to heal the wounds and for God to take away the bitterness and turn it into forgiveness.

Although the outcome can be positive, we cannot take episodes or seasons of betrayal lightly. Perhaps the reason betrayal hurts so much is because it thrives in the spaces where dependence binds us. For instance, children rely on parents not only for physical needs but also for emotional sustenance. When a parent betrays, the child grapples with conflicting emotions—acceptance of betrayal as a protective response to ensure safety or the possibility of future betrayals that erode self-esteem and emotional well-being.

Similarly, adults caught in toxic relationships—financially or socially dependent—face a cruel dilemma. Acknowledging betrayal could jeopardize their safety, so they bury the trauma. Memories blur, distorted by fear and necessity. The pain remains, festering beneath the surface.

In psychology, *attachment theory* underscores the roots of betrayal that stem from trauma. Our earliest bonds lay the ground-work for future relationships. Secure attachments foster trust, while insecure attachments breed instability. When betrayal strikes, the attachment bond fractures. The person who once held your emotional safety net becomes the source of pain. As such, betrayal tends to have lingering effects that, if not dealt with, can sabo-tage a person's ability to engage in meaningful, safe, healthy, and lasting relationships.

///////////////////////////////////

Betrayal was directly correlated to Joseph's God-size dreams.

///////

For Joseph, the pain must have been unbearable. He was on a mission from his father to check on his brothers. "When they saw him far off, even before he came near them, they conspired to kill him. Then they said to one another, 'Look, the dreamer is coming!'" (Genesis 37:18-19, author paraphrase). Did I read that correctly? They conspired to kill him because of the greatness embedded within him. Their desire to kill Joseph did not arise until *after* he shared his dreams. Their betrayal was directly correlated to his God-size dreams.

Could it be that some of the betrayals we experience are in direct proportion to the greatness within us? An act of betrayal from a parent to a child often speaks of the parent's inadequacy, not the child's shortcomings. As a matter of fact, I have seen parents betray their children because the emerging greatness demonstrated by the child reminds them of their own failures. I have witnessed individuals betrayed because a family member felt threatened by their success. Each person carries their own baggage, their own flaws, and their own choices. When someone betrays you, it reflects their character, not yours. Their actions stem from their own shortcomings, insecurities, and decisions.

As a person who has invested more than twenty years in pastoral ministry, I have experienced my share of betrayal. Again, why does it hurt so badly? Because it did not come from people I wasn't connected to. No! It came from people I had invested time, effort, and resources in. People I had mentored, shared meals with, trusted in leadership positions, and treated like family. Yet, in an instant, they betrayed my trust and affection. Like Joseph, I had to allow time to heal the wounds and eventually understand that what they meant for evil, God used for my good.

THE FLIP SIDE

Could there be a flip side to betrayal? Is there something positive that derives from the pain of betrayal that could have prevented you from spiraling into an emotional abyss of anger and resentment? I say there is! If we learn anything from the many who came before us and overcame betrayal, let it be that great things can come from it.

To understand the positive outcome of betrayal, let us look at Joseph's life backward. A hindsight perspective allows us the benefit of peeking into the success of others while we undergo similar challenges.

At first glance, it seems the dream would come to a screeching halt the moment Joseph is betrayed. Sold into slavery, he must now endure years of hardship before rising to prominence in Egypt. Yet, despite the cruelty he endured, Joseph's betrayal ultimately catalyzed positive change in his life that led him to fulfill his purpose in a remarkable way.

Joseph's betrayal could have spelled doom. Separated from his family and thrust into slavery, he faced numerous trials and tribulations. However, Joseph's resilience and unwavering faith allowed him to persevere through these challenges. Instead of succumbing to bitterness and despair, he remained steadfast in his belief that his life had a greater purpose. Somehow, he understood that betrayal was not the end of the story. He chose to become better instead of becoming bitter. How do we know that? We know that because he excelled at everything he did. Those are the actions of someone who has recognized that what was done to him did not have to tarnish his character, his actions, and, ultimately, his future. His brothers' actions spoke about *their* character. His actions spoke about his.

When we look at Joseph's life in hindsight, we don't ignore the horrors of what happened. We know from reading about the challenges he endured that his life was far from easy. Yet, his decision to maintain a position of personal integrity and resilience allowed what could have destroyed him to launch him into promotion. Somehow, he understood that betrayal was not the end of the story.

//

> ## What if we understood that our character and actions can advance our dreams and heal us at the same time?

////////

What about you? What will you do when you face betrayal—a hurt you didn't deserve? Could it be that if we are not careful, those hurts can paralyze our momentum toward the fulfillment of a God-size dream? What if we used the process as a path to prove our resilience instead? What if we understood that our character and actions can advance our dreams and heal us at the same time?

Let me provide you with three principles that can turn the bitter waters of betrayal into a more palatable taste of destiny. These principles can serve as models of forgiveness and redemption.

TIME

Someone once said that time, often personified as a great healer, has the subtle power to mend the wounds of betrayal. I agree! Unquestionably, when trust is broken, the initial shock and pain can seem insurmountable. Yet, as days turn into weeks and weeks into months, the intensity of this pain gradually diminishes. This is not to say that the memories fade away completely, but rather that their sharp edges are smoothed over by the passage of time.

The process of healing allows for introspection and growth. It can provide an opportunity to reassess your values and understand the depth of your resilience. As you navigate through the stages of grief and come to terms with betrayal, there is a newfound strength that emerges. This strength fosters a sense of self-reliance and confidence that may not have been fully developed before.

Moreover, time grants perspective. With it, you can see the betrayal as a single event in the grand scheme of life, rather than a defining moment. Remember, God-size dreams are awaiting fulfillment. This perspective is liberating, as it frees you to dream again, set new goals, and chase after what brings joy and fulfillment.

The lessons of betrayal become invaluable as you pursue your dreams. They serve as a guide to forming healthier relationships, setting boundaries, and choosing paths that align more closely with your aspirations. The gained wisdom acts as a compass, directing you toward a future that is not tainted by the past but rather informed by it.

Ultimately, time does not erase the past, but it allows the pain to transform it into a source of empowerment. It paves the way for achieving dreams, not in spite of the betrayal, but because of the growth that occurred as a result of it. In this way, time does not just heal; it also reveals a path forward, illuminated by the lessons of yesterday and the hopes of tomorrow.

RESILIENCE

Imagine a teenager, spoiled by his father, attempting to navigate a newfound journey of potential greatness. Is he ready to make those dreams become his reality? Or has his environment shielded him from turmoil? In the same way, could it be that the unprovoked and senseless act of betrayal launched Joseph into the school of resilience in preparation for the fulfillment of a dream that was much bigger than him?

> **Dreams, often fragile and elusive, thrive in the fertile soil of adversity.**

You and I are no different. At the moment of betrayal, the act may come as a devastating blow to an otherwise normal life. Yet, as painful as it may be, it tends to cultivate a root of resilience that grows to sustain us as we prepare for greatness.

Dreams, often fragile and elusive, thrive in the fertile soil of adversity. Such adversity is the by-product of betrayal. It forces us to confront our vulnerabilities, igniting a fire within—a determination to rise above the pain and forge ahead. Like a tree buffeted by fierce winds, we learn to bend without breaking, and resilience emerges as we face adversity head-on. In turn, resilience helps us to rebuild trust, forges inner strength, teaches us to redraw boundaries, and fuels transformation. Let's look at those descriptors in more detail.

Trust

How can you and I, like Joseph, rebuild trust after such a debilitating blow to a heart that was once full of emotional, trustworthy surrender? Trust shattered is like a mirror cracked. We pick up the shards and examine each jagged piece. Those pieces can cut through even the toughest of skin. They have the potential to cause us to bleed out emotionally. Conversely, through the power of resilience, we can learn to handle brokenness differently.

In this process, we can learn discernment—the ability to recognize genuine allies from those who merely wear masks. Resilience continues to bloom as we rebuild trust cautiously. We become adept at discerning intentions and navigating relationships with newfound wisdom. We begin to realize that these characteristics are essential to where we are headed. They are needed to fulfill the God-size dreams embedded within our soul. We come to realize that our dreams require trust—trust in ourselves, in others, and in the world around us, regardless of how difficult it may be.

Inner Strength

Who are we kidding? Betrayal leaves scars! Yet, they can become an ongoing reminder of the pain of familial and relational duplicity, *or* they can become reminders of our God-endowed resilience.

When we choose the latter, we emerge from the crucible with a steely resolve—an inner fortitude that refuses to yield. We are reminded that our dreams, like delicate glass sculptures, need this strength to withstand life's buffeting winds.

As you begin to lift up your head from the shame, guilt, confusion, and emotional drain that often comes from betrayal, the scars attempt to remind you of the act that so devastatingly interrupted your life. Yet, in a still, small voice, resilience whispers, "You survived! You thrived!" Our dreams, too, begin to speak. They beckon us to rise up stronger than ever and mold our pain into purpose!

Redraw Boundaries

My mother's unconfrontational demeanor set the standard for a young boy afraid to displease anyone. Both my father and mother were bridge-builders. Not in a literal sense. They strived to build familial relationships with extended family and friends alike. As positive of a trait as that was, it blinded me from people's ulterior motives. Like Joseph, I often shared dreams with people who did not have my best interest in mind. So, when betrayal knocked on my door, I was ill-prepared to handle its emotional blows. Yet, through time, betrayal taught me to redraw boundaries.

I learned to say no and realized that it was okay! We say no to protect our hearts. We recognize that vulnerability isn't weakness—it's courage. I learned—and I pray you do too—that our dreams require boundaries. We guard them fiercely and say no to distractions, naysayers, and self-doubt. Resilience sharpens our focus, aligning our actions with our aspirations.

Transformation

When our aspirations begin to arise, we affirm the idea that betrayal is a chrysalis—a cocoon of transformation. We emerge with wings of resilience, ready to soar. Our dreams, like caterpillars, undergo metamorphosis. Betrayal fuels this transformation. We shed old beliefs, embrace uncertainty, and emerge as dream-chasers—resilient, relentless, and ready to move on toward new dimensions! I don't care if betrayal has caused you to inch your way through life like a caterpillar. As the dreams embedded within continue to emerge, let me remind you that you were meant to fly!

FORGIVENESS

Ultimately, Joseph's experiences in Egypt provided him with the opportunity to reconcile with his brothers. When they came seeking food during the famine, Joseph revealed himself to them and forgave them for their past transgressions. This act of forgiveness not only healed the rift between Joseph and his brothers but also allowed for the reunification of his family. In hindsight, Joseph recognized that his betrayal and subsequent journey to Egypt were all part of a larger plan. Through his trials and triumphs, he fulfilled his purpose of saving his family and the nation of Egypt from destruction. His story serves as a testament to the power of resilience, forgiveness, and faith in overcoming adversity and achieving destiny. As it was with Joseph, may it also be with you!

8

FAILURE IS NOT THE END

"It is not whether you failed; it is whether you can overcome failure and keep moving."
—C. Olmeda

"It's fine to celebrate success but it is more important to heed the lessons of failure."
—Bill Gates

Failure. The word itself carries a weight, a sting that lingers long after the event. It's not merely falling short of a goal; it is the echo of missed opportunities, shattered dreams, and the gnawing fear that we might never rise again. When failure strikes, it injects venom into our veins. The initial pain subsides, but the residue remains.

As if the lingering residue was not enough to prick at our conscience and remind us of our mistakes, complacency—the silent accomplice—creeps in and whispers, "Stay here. It's safer. Don't risk again." We settle into mediocrity, wrapping ourselves in a cocoon of excuses, to the extent that the sting numbs our ambition, and we become ineffective.

Failure has the propensity to breed self-doubt. So much so that, like a looping song that never ends, we replay the scenes, the missed shots, the rejected manuscripts, the faltering speeches. Each replay intensifies the emotions, prompting us to question our worth and abilities. The sting morphs into a chorus of "not good enough," so convincing that it can paralyze any intention to move forward. But it is here that I remind you that failure is not the end.

STEWARDSHIP

Certainly, it is easier to say that failure is not the end when I am not the one experiencing the agonizing and paralyzing sting that often comes as an outgrowth of failure. Not that I have not experienced countless moments of failure, when, I too, thought there was no way out. But I get it. I completely understand the overwhelming sense of isolation and desperation that comes with failure. I can't tell you how many times I have heard someone say, "You have no idea what I am going through! I don't see a way out!" At that moment, that may be the absolute truth. They don't see a way out. However, I can also serve as a testament that there is! There is a way out!

Let's peek into the life of Chris (name changed for anonymity), a young man for whom I have had the pleasure of witnessing firsthand how failure could have served as a devastating blow of defeat to him, his family, and his business. Yet somehow, without being privy to the model set forth throughout this manuscript, he knew there was another dimension beyond failure awaiting his arrival.

When I met Chris, by his own admission, he could barely read or write cohesively. He was a young, single father looking for love in all the wrong places. This young man had been promoted from one grade to another throughout his high school years, not based on his academic aptitude, but because he was great at football. That potential career, however, came to a screeching halt when he chose relationships, partying, and money-making over football scholarships.

One night, after a church service, I could tell from the desperation in his voice that he no longer desired to spiral down that path of dissolution and despair. So, there he was, desiring to seek God and turn his life around . . . and that he did! The proverbial night and day difference I witnessed Chris go through was, in every sense, transformational. So, one would think that with such a transformation would come a series of accomplishments, not failure. For several years, it was exactly that.

Over the next few years, Chris got married, launched a business from the trunk of his car, and, with fear and trembling (as he would describe it), enrolled in theology classes. Did I mention that he did not know how to effectively read or write? So, unquestionably, pursuing unchartered territory for anyone in his family or prior generations was not only challenging but terrifying for him. Yet, he pushed through. He pushed through with resilience even while afraid (that could be its own chapter). If you met Chris, he would admit to you that he learned how to read and write in the church while taking one theology class after another.

As his faith increased, so did his resilience. He went from working out of his trunk to securing a partnership with a network of dealerships through which he could run his business out of their facilities. At a glance, he was living the American dream. He was now married with children, a homeowner, and a thriving business owner. Even greater, the opportunity presented itself for him to open his own location. He could now have his clients go to his business location rather than meet him at different dealerships.

//

He felt that chasing money may work for some people, but God had different plans for him.

////////

For several years, he added additional services that would benefit his clients. As the business grew, so did his ambition. He would later admit, "I started to take ownership of what I should have been a steward of!" As he would analyze how far he had come, he would say, "This is only the beginning. If I work harder and devote more time, then one location can turn into another, and another, and another!" Quite frankly, there is nothing wrong with that! Many people have accomplished similar feats in their lifetime. However, for Chris, it became a consuming desire for success. "If I had to choose between attending a mid-week Bible study from which my initial fuel and fervor derived or seizing an opportunity for more money, I would choose the latter," he would regretfully admit. "That may work for some people, but that was not the God-size dream for me," he suggested as we conversed about his journey. He felt that chasing money may work for some people, but God had different plans for him.

Through a series of challenges and what he would consider the perfect storm, Chris's business began to disintegrate. "I didn't know exactly what was happening, but I knew I had not stewarded—I had not managed—the dream God had given me to the best of my ability. I became enamored with the dream instead of the Dream-Giver!" The pain of regret was evident in his tone. As he shared the painful loss of his business location, leading him to bankruptcy, I could tell Chris was not well. His attempt to remain calm and positive was overshadowed by the sense of failure that would consistently surface above his attempt to project positive rhetoric. He was hurting. At that moment, he felt he had failed, and there was no way out.

As Chris navigated this painful journey, he thought of what his boys would think of him. Would he lose his home? What would his wife think? What would those he mingled with at the church think of his faith and dependence on God? Would he be criticized by those he had shared his success with? Now, he had to explain how most of his success was nonexistent.

Like Chris, none of us are exempt from similar emotions. As the sting of failure burns within our subconscious thoughts and its effects spill out in what we say—whether intentionally or not—the thought of a way out often evades us. All we see is the outcome of what once was. The humiliation can be enough to bury any potential attempt at mustering up enough courage and resilience to forget the past and move forward. It is not that simple. But as I have stated before, time becomes our best friend. The pain begins to fade, and the thought of a new dimension begins to emerge on the horizon.

For Chris, his failure turned into fuel. "I reevaluated my priorities and decided to depend on the One who had given me my dreams in the first place," he later confessed! "My pain became fuel to encourage others who had or were going through difficult times!" As I took time to listen to his story, the principles he taught exhilarated me. He would say things like, "I had to realize that all I had accomplished was part of God's plan for my life. I was only a steward, not the owner. In an odd kind of way, I understood that had I continued down that path, I would have limited myself from the greater things God had in store for me!"

Perhaps that wouldn't make sense for many unless they knew the rest of his story. Because if you are anything like me, you will not find anything wrong with the kind of success Chris experienced. I began to understand that however great his success was, the God-size dreams for his life had more to do with impact than with money.

As I ponder that principle, I am quickly reminded of the many people I have met and heard of who have achieved great success by financial standards yet felt miserable. People who lost relationships, sacrificed their children on the altar of success, so to speak, and lost years of intentional impact in the lives of others. Although grand, their success could not compare to the impact associated with God-size dreams—the kind of impact that creates a ripple effect not only in the life of the person living out the dream but also in the lives of family members and people in general for generations to come.

For Chris, failure was not the end. He became more spiritually focused than ever. As the months turned into years, his business started to thrive again. Money was no longer his focus. He wanted to build a business he could pass down to his older son. The lessons he learned catapulted him into mentoring the next generation of men to become stewards of God-size dreams and not owners blinded by success.

So many of us become enamored with a taste of God-size dreams and miss out on the bigger picture.

If you met Chris today, you would meet a credentialed minister who, in recent months, has been traveling as a consultant with a well-known international organization, meeting with pastors and leaders in preparation for national Christian crusades that attract thousands upon thousands of people. His business continues to thrive as his older son takes the lead while his father travels, fulfilling God-size dreams.

So many of us, like Chris, become enamored with a taste of God-size dreams and miss out on the bigger picture. (I will elaborate on this through one of the upcoming dimensions.) We begin to experience levels of success and stop implementing the principles that got us there in the first place. We attempt to become masters of what we should be stewards of. We try to take ownership of what we should be managing.

LESSONS LEARNED

Success often blinds us to what truly matters. When everything seems to go smoothly, we prioritize achievement, wealth, and reputation. Conversely, failure has a way of recalibrating our focus. It strips away the superficial and reveals the eternal. We learn that true blessings lie in our relationship with the Dream-Giver and the impact we have on others.

> **Failure provides a crash course on wisdom.**

Let us turn the tables on failure and extract lessons that will catapult us into destiny rather than eternal guilt and condemnation. As we do, we will begin to realize that failure toughens our resolve. It teaches us to get up after falling and to keep moving forward despite setbacks. As such, it can paradoxically become the catalyst for growth, wisdom, and the pursuit of God-size dreams.

When we encounter failure, whether due to our own mistakes or external circumstances, it provides valuable lessons that shape our character and propel us toward greater achievements. Failure provides a crash course on wisdom. We analyze what went wrong, identify our mistakes, and adjust our approach. King Solomon, renowned for his wisdom, wrote, "For a righteous *man* may fall seven times And rise again" (Proverbs 24:16, NKJV).

Never forget that *the Giver* of your God-size dreams specializes in turning failures into victories. Remember our protagonist, Joseph?

His brothers sold him into slavery, yet he later became a ruler in Egypt. When the time came to face them, he declared, "You meant evil against me, *but* God meant it for good" (Genesis 50:20, NKJV). How about we metaphorically take the same approach? How about we look at those past or present failures and declare the same, "You meant evil against me, but God meant it for good!" What could have pushed me to drown in a sea of despair has given me new life to see things differently. When you understand that there is another dimension looming on the horizon, you will understand that failure is not the end of your story. Instead, it becomes a step in the right direction!

9

WHEN TIME BETRAYS

"Your dream isn't over; you're just being prepared for its fulfillment."
—C. Olmeda

Dreams often emerge like glistening stars shimmering with promise and possibility. These dreams, audacious in nature, ignite our hearts and propel us forward. Yet, as we journey toward their fulfillment, we encounter a silent adversary: time. When our God-size dreams remain unfulfilled, it is easy to feel betrayed by time. We wonder why our dream—the vision we carry within us—has not materialized. As time passes, we question our worthiness, our abilities, and even God's faithfulness. As the calendar pages relentlessly turn, we find ourselves standing at the intersection of longing and reality.

Imagine our protagonist, Joseph. As a young man, he has received dreams that translate into greatness. Although he cannot decipher their outcome with precision, they have become a blueprint for something exceeding his wildest imagination. Yet, as the years unfolded, they told a different story. As the days passed, instead of fulfillment, he faced betrayal. As the days turned into months, instead of fulfillment, he faced slavery. As the months turned into years, instead of fulfillment, he faced imprisonment. Repeatedly, time seemed to mock him, and there was nothing he could do to change the outcome. Joseph had to ride the journey of time with its bumps and bruises and brace for its impact.

DON'T STOP THE ROLL

I am reminded of my instructor's admonition while I was enrolled in a motorcycle safety course. He said, "There is nothing like riding along a beautiful country road on a sunny day, enjoying the wind in your face and the feeling of freedom." He was right! I still don't know what it is about a few guys gathering early in the morning, revving up their Harley-Davidsons (you can't refer to them as just motorcycles), and like a sacred procession, riding in unison along some country road with the sweet sound of loud pipes resounding in their ears like the sound of a sweet melody bringing a smile to their faces. I digress!

However beautiful that experience is, the instructor suggested that although he did not wish it upon any of us, those rides could take a turn for the worse. As such, he was preparing us. The slipping of the motorcycle on gravel or someone abruptly cutting you off are a couple of the endless reasons why a motorcycle driver could lose control, fall off a motorcycle, and roll down the road. "If that were to ever happen," he cautioned us with a stern voice, "do not stiffen your body! You will break more bones than you ever imagined!"

Immediately, I thought, *What am I supposed to do, play dead?*

As if he could read my thoughts, he proceeded, "Play dead! Keep your body as flaccid as possible and just roll. Let the momentum take you until you come to a stop!"

I received the admonition and interpreted it into my own words: "Don't fight the process!"

//

When time, as a betrayer, interrupts the course of your dreams, don't try to stop the roll.

//////////

I didn't realize that fighting the process would cause more damage than simply rolling limply to a complete stop. The same is true of your dreams. One day, you could be *riding* along, enjoying the journey, and the next moment, you're rolling down the pro-verbial road of pain, suffering, failure, and betrayal. The more you fight it, the more painful it becomes. To fight the process is to attempt to alleviate the pain before the healing process has taken its course. It is to ignore the suffering, allow the guilt of betrayal to stagnate you, and attempt to fight your betrayers. It becomes an exercise in futility. You end up tired, frustrated, weighed down, and depleted.

Instead, when time, as a betrayer, interrupts the course of your dreams, don't try to stop the roll. Unlike the painful outcome of an unavoidable motorcycle accident, the bumps and bruises associ-ated with the interruption of dreams usually come with valuable lessons. For Joseph, what seemed like the interruption of a dream became the waiting room of preparation. The process taught him resilience, humility, and trust. His dreams had not been forgotten. They were being refined! In hindsight, what may have been misconstrued as interruptions became a convergence of factors bringing together circumstances, relationships, and skills that served to fuel his dreams and witness their fulfillment. It is God's way of connecting the dots.

CONNECT THE DOTS

As a child, I often enjoyed connecting the dots. Although they were not dots, per se, I had an affinity toward a special kind of coloring book filled with images that were unrecognizable unless you connected the dots. The dots were not dots after all. ("Connect the dots" is a figure of speech.) They were letters or numbers. As you progressively connected each subsequent letter or number, you would begin to see the clearer picture the illustrator intended to reveal. Quite often, I could make out the picture before completing the process—albeit not in complete detail. Other times, I thought I knew what the picture was, but once the dots were connected, I would soon realize I had been mistaken.

God-size dreams and God-size visions are often like those connect-the-dots pictures. We often think we know what the picture looks like until we are faced with the realization that until all the dots are connected, we will not get a clear understanding of the Dream-Giver's intended purpose.

LOSING IT ALL

Most of us are familiar with the idiom, "Hindsight is 20/20." This simply means that we often have the ability to see things more clearly after they have happened, rather than when they first happened. The stories of Abraham and Joseph are not exempt from such an idiom. It's quite easy for me to extrapolate lessons from their historic journeys in a succinct manner because I already know the outcome. But what about the person going through the process who has not seen what the completed picture looks like? All they have to go on is the effects of whatever the journey brings as it unravels.

There is a woman in the Bible who fits this model to perfection. We are introduced to her in the fourth chapter of 2 Kings. She is referred to as the Shunammite, as she lived in the village of Shunem in the territory of Issachar, about twenty miles from Mt. Carmel. She was wealthy and hospitable. She and her husband became aware of a holy man—a prophet named Elisha—who would occasionally pass through Shunem. Through a prompting unbeknownst to us, they decided to extend hospitality to him.

Their hospitality went beyond an afternoon lunch or evening meal. They went as far as building a separate guest room for him to stay in. They furnished it and provided meals for him whenever he passed through their village. Undoubtedly, this woman's kindness and extravagant hospitality demonstrated her generosity and reverence toward Elisha.

Touched by her hospitality, the holy man desired to reciprocate her actions in kind. He asked her what he could do for her. She humbly declined any specific request, seemingly content with her life. Elisha's servant, Gehazi, noticed that the woman had no children. Despite her silence on this matter, Elisha discerned her unspoken desire for a son. Perhaps she had buried any dream of having a child as months had turned into years, and for untold reasons, she remained childless. As God's representative, Elisha boldly promised her that she would have a son within a year.

Earlier, I suggested that through a prompting unbeknownst to us, this woman had decided to extend hospitality to Elisha. What if that is how dreams are birthed? What if dreams are birthed by following an internal prompting that extends beyond normal, everyday behavior? As we follow this woman's journey and the supernatural occurrences that ensued, we realize that her prompting, and ultimately her actions, were part of a God-size dream she had initially buried. Yet, through an act of obedience to an internal prompting, that dream came alive in ways that exceeded her expectations.

If you have followed the path of this fifth-dimension model thus far, you have noticed that God-size dreams do not follow a straight progression of fulfillment without any interruptions, failures, betrayal, or pain. The Shunammite was no exception.

True to Elisha's word, the woman bore a son. Although this miraculous gift brought several years of immense joy to her life, tragically, the child fell ill one day and died suddenly. Devastated, she laid her son's body on Elisha's bed and sought the prophet's help. Elisha prayed fervently, and God restored the boy's life. Within a short period of time, this woman experienced great loss *and* miraculous restoration. Like watching a ping-pong match and witnessing the back-and-forth movement of a small ball, this woman's life mimicked the same phenomenon: a buried dream followed by a prompting to show hospitality to Elisha. For a short moment, it seems as if her generosity had been reciprocated via the awakening of a dream for a child, only to witness his death within a few short years. As she navigated that complexity of emotions, she experienced a miracle. It would be wonderful to say that her miracle was followed by a break from hardship, but that was not the case. The story did not end there.

Sadly, not too long after, the prophet counseled the woman to leave her city because a famine would cover the land for seven years. "So the woman arose and did according to the saying of the man of God, and she went with her household and dwelt in the land of the Philistines seven years" (2 Kings 8:2, NKJV).

When does it end? How can someone demonstrate such generosity yet experience one chaotic moment after another? Maybe you, too, have felt that way before. I have! Undoubtedly, these are the moments that prompt you to think whether God-size dreams become a reality or whether the hope of their fulfillment is simply a figment of our imagination. Understanding her psychological trauma or how she processed her inevitable journey throughout her seven years in a land not her own would certainly have been beneficial. Did she have moments when she wanted to give up? Was she concerned about how she would provide for a son she had not asked for? Perhaps for many years, she desired to have him. Yet now, considering her circumstances, could she feel that she would have been better without him? Despite the unanswered questions, I am thrilled that the story did not end there.

WHEN THE DOTS CONNECT

In the eighth year, after the seven-year famine was over, the Shunammite decided to return from the land of the Philistines and appeal to the king for her house and her land. Now, I must caution you to brace yourself because this is where this entire story comes together.

//

> # When God-size dreams exceed personal limitations, there are no coincidences!

/////////

Keep in mind that the days were long gone since the Shunammite had demonstrated generosity to Elisha. She had experienced life's unsettling instability to the extent that although her son's life had been spared, she had lost her home and land. Yet, as she made her way to plead her case before the king, *coincidentally*, Elisha's servant Gehazi happened to be engaged in a conversation with the king. *Coincidentally*, the king was in the middle of questioning him about Elisha's life. *Coincidentally*, Gehazi was in the process of telling the king about how Elisha had brought to life a woman's son who lived in Shunem. And *coincidentally*, guess who walked in at that precise moment? Yes, the Shunammite and her son! About whom Gehazi exclaimed, "This is the woman, and this is her son!"

If you have not yet caught on, please understand that when God-size dreams exceed personal limitations, there are no coincidences! What are the chances of Gehazi having a conversation with the king at the same exact time the woman arrived to appeal for her home and her land? The only reason he spoke about a woman whose son Elisha brought back to life was that, years earlier, the Shunammite followed a prompting to demonstrate generosity to a man she honored. What if she had ignored that prompting? What if she had justified it with, "It's too much work and will cost too much money to build a room for this man"? What if she had limited herself to simply serving him a meal and not dreaming beyond her everyday style of living?

She did not ignore her initial prompting! Although she could not decipher with clarity what the full picture of her life would look like as she experienced a roller coaster of emotions, one thing we know for certain: the Dream-Giver was connecting the dots all along! So much so, that the king appointed an officer to restore all that was hers and all the proceeds of the field from the day she had left until her return.

> **Rest assured that as you trust the process, the dots are being connected, and the dream will not disappoint.**

This teaches us that obedience is not an option; it is a mandate. We must be sensitive to the promptings, even when we do not have the foresight of what's ahead. It will require us to follow the path to meet people, make connections, and be at the right place at the right time. We must understand that heeding the promptings we get sets off a series of events that lead to fulfillment.

How about you? Have you felt like the Shunammite? Have you experienced a journey that has obscured what the final outcome of your life would look like? Have you been on the verge of experiencing the outcome of what you thought was a God-size dream, only to be confronted by a setback? Let me encourage you to

surrender to the process. Don't fight the process! Like the motor-
cyclist, you may end up with more brokenness than you could
have imagined. Instead, trust the process. Rest assured that as you
trust the process, the dots are being connected, and the dream will
not disappoint.

10

LIVING WITH FAILURE
AND SUCCESS

"Consequences and success can live together."
—C. Olmeda

Take a deep breath! You made it past the dimension of failure, past the dimension of betrayal! Others did not. Some have succumbed to the devastating blow of failure's brutal attack and never recovered the resilience to get back up and press forward to a new dimension. Others, scarred by betrayal's deeply embedded wounds, have remained stuck in unforgiveness, anger, and hatred. That is not to say that the second dimension fades away into the past without leaving behind residue. It does. It often leaves behind consequences that must be dealt with even while moving into a new dimension.

Consequences are the outcomes of our choices and actions. They shape our lives in significant ways. As we make it through the second dimension, we do not move forward without recognizing that, oftentimes, our decisions lead to unintended results. How many of us have hurt others, damaged relationships, or faced personal setbacks? As we make every attempt to move forward, we cannot do so without the consequences of our actions tagging along.

If the consequences of your actions are going to walk in tandem with the progression of your dreams, then something must change. You must change the way you perceive their effect on your life. You must change your perspective about the role those consequences play. They may have been affected by your actions, but they will not be your master.

CONVICTION OR CONDEMNATION

Growing up in a loving home, though legalistic and dogmatic in nature, instilled a complex set of emotions in me that I had to decipher and work through in my adult years. Please do not misinterpret my analysis for criticism. I am who I am today, in part, because of the God-fearing, caring parents who loved me unconditionally. However, they, too, had adapted to a rigid lifestyle of religious adherence that left very little room for questioning the established order.

For instance, I grew up believing that guilt was God's way of showing me that I had violated divine standards. When you live long enough with constant reminders of what you have done wrong, you can easily develop a neurotic, false sense of guilt. That guilt can stem from your parental upbringing or a conscience misguided by an unhealthy level of rules and regulations. It may not necessarily derive from the violation of a divine standard. As such, it condemns. It serves as a debilitating and depleting voice that reminds you of everything you did wrong and why progress has evaded you.

Have you met anyone like that? People stuck and debilitated by guilt? I have met and spoken to dozens of people debilitated by guilt. They become paralyzed by succumbing to the voices that tell them, "You're not good enough!" "You will never recover from what you did!" or "You will always be limited by your past mistakes!" The feeling becomes so overwhelmingly belittling that they live oppressed beneath their own feelings of guilt and shame, unable to see past their mistakes and into a better future. That level of guilt breeds condemnation.

Conversely, there is the guilt that fuels conviction. The *Merriam-Webster Dictionary* defines conviction as "the state of being convinced of error or compelled to admit the truth."[2] When you are convinced of misalignment or compelled to come clean, so to speak, then that behavior should lead to freedom, not condemnation. You are no longer bound by an erroneous belief or hidden lies. Instead, the conviction becomes a reminder of what once held you back, not a lack of freedom or a constraint to future progress.

MARKED IN RED

Let me give you an example. I admit that despite my academic advancements, I thoroughly dislike test-taking. I would research, engage in qualitative and quantitative investigations, examine data, and write all day long if I had to. But do not make me take a

---

2 Merriam-Webster.com Dictionary, s.v. "conviction," accessed August 5, 2024, https://www.merriam-webster.com/dictionary/conviction.

test. I will do it, but not without breaking out in a sweat and over-thinking the material beyond what is necessary. Even when I know that I know what I am supposed to know (Did you get that?), I still second-guess my knowledge. I often wonder, *Why?* (Maybe I should schedule a session with my psychotherapist wife.)

Perhaps it stems from the emotional scars associated with the color red. For reasons that never made sense to me, I still remember that whenever I took a test in grade school, the only thing highlighted in red were the answers I got wrong. Let's say I took a twenty-question test and got eighteen questions right and two questions wrong. The only highlights that would surface from the test once the teacher returned it were the two questions I had gotten wrong, highlighted in red. Talk about conditioning. I began to associate red with failure. Why not change that association and highlight the eighteen questions I got *right* in red?

> **When guilt fuels condemnation, it promotes isolation, low self-esteem, rejection, and even self-inflicted punishment. But when guilt fuels conviction, it catalyzes change.**

You might think differently. In the same situation, you may think, *Whew, I am just glad I passed the test!* Well, that is not my story. I often thought, *I cannot believe I got that question wrong! I knew that answer!* or worse yet, *I don't remember ever reading that in my notes! What was I thinking?* I should have been celebrating the fact that I had just received a ninety on a twenty-question test. Instead, I felt frustrated and often condemned by what went wrong. Why? Simply because what was highlighted in red was the failure and not the success. Highlighted in red was what was wrong instead of what was right. Perhaps for many of us, the red marks were the beginning of believing that life would highlight everything that went wrong with little room to celebrate everything that went right! This is why, as a professor, I try to make every effort to highlight my students' achievements in red, followed by an affirmation.

When guilt fuels condemnation, it promotes isolation, low self-esteem, rejection, and even self-inflicted punishment. But when guilt fuels conviction, it catalyzes change.

What if, instead of highlighting failure, we focus on the lessons that come from those daunting moments of failure and betrayal? I am not suggesting we ignore the consequences of poor decisions, mistakes, or even, at times, ignorance. Quite the contrary! I am suggesting that if emotional baggage is going to embed itself in the advancement of my dreams, then I will control its effect on my life. Not vice versa! When consequences tag along, I will use them as reminders that:

- I will not repeat those actions again.
- The greatness that lies before me is infinitely greater than the challenges behind me.
- Failure is not the end. It is an opportunity to try again with more wisdom!
- Betrayal cannot detain the fulfillment of God-size dreams.

SELF-SUFFICIENCY

What if I took this a step further and suggested that the consequences of failure and betrayal can become a framework of checks and balances? A way to keep us from believing we are self-sufficient and grandiose! Considering that success has a way of promoting pretentious behavior, consequences may serve as a reminder that we have the propensity to ruin what could have been perfect. It keeps us humble!

THE DECEIVER

Let us look at a character whose very name means "supplanter"— someone who seizes, circumvents, or usurps. We read about his scheming behavior in the Bible in Genesis 25 and onward: a young man named Jacob who took advantage of his older brother's hunger pangs. After his brother, Esau, had worked all day, he came home ready for a home-cooked meal. Jacob offered him a bowl of pottage in exchange for his birthright. Offering up one's birthright was not taken lightly in Jacob's time. Its long-term ramifications would bear unimaginable consequences that neither party was prepared to face. Yet, Esau made the unequal trade, nonetheless.

As if deceiving his brother was not enough, Jacob also deceived his father. When the time came for his dying father to declare a blessing over his older son Esau, Jacob disguised himself as his brother and deceived their father into thinking he was blessing the older of the two.

Jacob had a moment to reconsider his actions—multiple moments, at that. At one point, his father, old and blind, asked Jacob one more time before blessing him, "Are you really my son Esau?" to which Jacob replied, "I am" (Genesis 27:24, NKJV).

Isn't that like many of us? How many times have we made a decision that led to wayward action or questionable behavior, fully aware of the proverbial door of escape—the door we could have exited if we had made a better decision? Yet, for reasons too complex to decipher here, we move forward, knowing that the action taken was not the right one.

It was no different for Jacob. His father blessed him. He probably thought he would live happily ever after as he walked away with his father's blessing! Yet, once his brother found out what he had done, he vowed to kill him. So terrible was the familial chaos that ensued that Jacob had to leave everything behind and flee for his life.

Despite such devastation—albeit self-inflicted—Jacob arrived at a certain place where he fell asleep and had a vision after running all day. In the vision, he saw a ladder with angels ascending and descending from heaven. At the top of the ladder, he saw *the Lord*, who spoke to him and assured him:

> *I am the Lord God of Abraham your father and the God of Isaac; the land on which you lie I will give to you and your descendants. Also your descendants shall be as the dust of the earth; you shall spread abroad to the west and the east, to the north and the south; and in you and in your seed all the families of the earth shall be blessed. Behold, I am with you and will keep you wherever you go, and will bring you back to this land; for I will not leave you until I have done what I have spoken to you.*
> *—Genesis 28:13-15 (NKJV)*

Are we talking about the same person here? Is God talking to the same Jacob whose brother was trying to kill him for deceiving him? Are we referring to the same Jacob who, apparently, with no remorse, lied to his father? Indeed, we are! So, is God ignoring all of Jacob's failures? After reading such a profound declaration of blessing, one would think that God is indeed turning a blind eye to Jacob's lapse in moral judgment. That is until you read the rest of the story.

The rest of the story is filled with principles from the law of sowing and reaping. What Jacob has sown in deceit, he reaps through deceit at the hands of his uncle. Jacob has to work seven years for the hand of Rachel, a woman who would become his wife. At the appointed time, instead of receiving Rachel to be his wife, he is given Leah, Rachel's older sister. Consequently, he must work another seven years for Rachel. From his marriages to his livestock to work demands, it seems like Jacob experiences one deception after another; one betrayal after another. Not to mention, he is still living in fear of his brother's revenge.

In what seems like a convoluted, existential dichotomy stemming from Jacob's life journey via historical prose, we come to realize that while Jacob is dealing with the consequences of his actions, he is simultaneously witnessing the realization of the words *the Lord* declared to him in that *certain place*.

Truthfully, the more I ponder Jacob's journey, the more I am at a loss for words. Why? Because at first glance, when I read of his accumulation of wealth—while on the run, no less—I immediately attribute it to hard work. I attribute it to diligence and resilience until I am reminded of the promise given to him during his vision of heaven. This is not simply Jacob at work but a God-size dream being fulfilled despite Jacob's shortcomings. It is his consequence and his success journeying in tandem.

Imagine if Jacob had succumbed to a life of emotional paralysis. What if he had dismissed the vision as a late-night nightmare signaling disqualification because of his moral deficiency? No! Jacob moved forward *while* dealing with the consequences. And if we were to believe that Jacob brushed his deceit under the proverbial carpet and moved on with life as if nothing had ever happened, we would be sadly mistaken. For years, even while witnessing success, he dealt with the fear of meeting his brother.

Jacob devised a plan to meet his brother. He sent servants, gifts, and messages and even prayed in an attempt to not lose his life at the hands of a vengeful brother. As he awaited the return of his servants, wondering what news they would bring back from his brother, Jacob was left alone. While alone, a *Man* wrestled with him. When this divine figure noticed He could not prevail against him, he disjointed Jacob's hip and left him with a limp (Genesis 32:24-25). He proceeded to ask Jacob, "What is your name?" to which he obviously replied, "Jacob!" The man replied, "Your name shall no longer be called Jacob, but Israel, for you have struggled with God and with men, and have prevailed" (Genesis 32:27-28, NKJV).

This is the first time we are made privy to Jacob's ongoing struggle. We knew it all along from reading the text. But now we are told that despite Jacob's success, he has been living in a perpetual struggle. And as if that was not enough, he now walks with a limp and still fears meeting his brother.

Yet, just as his name has changed, so have his circumstances. Time has healed his brother's heart. When the time came to see each other face-to-face, God had heard Jacob's prayers of remorse and repentance, and familial forgiveness ensued. The consequences of his actions had been a constant companion but not enough to detain him from seeing the fulfillment of God-size dreams.

> ## Consequences may be your companion, but they will never be your master.

Success does not mean the absence of consequences. Nor does it mean that everything in your life will perfectly align as you progress and eventually experience the fulfillment of a God-size dream. Instead, it means:

- Like Jacob, you may experience success while grappling with fear.
- Like the apostle Paul in the Bible, you may become one of the most influential and prolific writers while dealing with an agonizing thorn in your flesh.
- Like David in the Bible, you may have to develop resilience and grow into God's purpose for your life while being chased, robbed, and demoted as you prove yourself worthy of that promotion in which you were called.

I once heard someone suggest, "As the dawn of every day breaks the silence of the night, get up, dress up, show up, and never give up!" Despite the dimension of failure and betrayal, I remind you once again: a greater dimension is looming on the horizon. Failure is not the end. Betrayal is not the end. Consequences may be your companion, but they will never be your master.

As you move forward past this heart-wrenching dimension, let me remind you that once you get a taste of what the fulfillment of your dreams can look like, there is no turning back. You press forward, knowing that your shortcomings will never be big enough to limit the fulfillment of God-size dreams. Let's journey together as we move to the third dimension.

3RD DIMENSION

TASTE

DREAMS & VISIONS

FAILURE OR BETRAYAL

TASTE

11

IT'S ONLY A TASTE

"Some miss out on abundance because they settle for a taste."
—C. Olmeda

I still remember the feeling! The feeling of anticipation! That feeling you get when you know you are on the brink of experiencing something powerful—something you have been expecting, yet the mystery of the unknown becomes overwhelming.

Whom will she look like? Will she be a healthy baby?

It had been a grueling four years for my wife and me. After two ectopic pregnancies and a roller coaster of emotions, my wife was about to be induced, and we would welcome our firstborn into the world. Nothing in this world compares to that moment. The miracle of life. The beauty of a woman carrying a child through birth while having navigated the ever-changing journey of physical, emotional, and hormonal changes. Nothing compares to it. That moment would make any man buckle at the knees.

Even as I write this, I chuckle at the memory of my ignorant demeanor as she pushed our baby into this world. At that moment, lying in the hospital bed, none of my wife's sacrifices crossed my mind. Instead, I stood on the margins, simply looking to reap the rewards of joy and exhilaration in welcoming our first daughter. My wife and I laugh about this now as she shares her thoughts about my fatherly theatrics: "As I laid there looking and feeling like I had been through a war," she quips, "all my husband could do was grin from ear to ear and follow the nurses as they scooped the baby away for a health check and proper cleaning. Hello! What about me?" (Hopefully, my unrehearsed exhilaration of experiencing the miracle of life unfolding right before my eyes and witnessing God bless us with a beautiful baby girl will justify my ignorant behavior.)

This miracle of life has been life-changing for many families in ways that have become an answered prayer. For others, what has been life-changing has been their inability to conceive. Somewhere along the spectrum, between those who can and those who cannot, lie several other complications, from unexpected pregnancies to undesired pregnancies and everything in between. My objective here is not to highlight one over the other or pass judgment on another person's circumstances. I pray for all families who long to have a child and cannot. I pray that, like some of the women in the Bible, they, too, would experience the miracle of life in whatever way deemed possible.

For my wife and me, everything changed in an instant. The pain and frustration of multiple lost pregnancies were now a distant memory. Any struggles we experienced outside of childbearing or growing a family seemed insignificant. We were holding a miracle, and nothing else mattered.

I wonder if that is how Abraham and Sarah felt as they welcomed Isaac. The promise God gave Abraham overshadowed his failure with Hagar. In reality, the complex consequences of that less-than-sound decision had not altogether vanished. For a moment in time, the couple basked in the taste of something greater than they could have ever imagined. An impossibility had turned into the beginning of a miracle that would change the world. Any success they had witnessed up to that point dwarfed in comparison to that moment. In Isaac, they received a taste of a promise, and their lives as they knew it would never be the same again.

WHY A TASTE?

A taste? Why do I suggest that Isaac was only a taste of a promise? Was he not the fulfillment? At first glance, it appears that way until we revisit the initial promise: "Look up at the sky and count the stars," Abram, "if indeed you can count them . . . so shall your offspring be" (Genesis 15:5, NIV). But let's not get ahead of ourselves. Just because Isaac was just a taste of what was to come does not mean that Abraham and Sarah could not, and should not, have basked in the joy of receiving something (or someone) they had lost hope of receiving. This was indeed a move into a new dimension.

> **A taste of what is to come has been given to you as a reminder that the dream is still alive.**

Finally, the dimension of failure has come to an end. (At least for now. I will revisit this in the fifth dimension chapters.) This is key to understanding each dimension's progression. There comes a time when, even if you experience the consequences of past mistakes, you must be open to holding firmly to your initial God-size vision—albeit as a taste. Many bury their God-size dream under the weight of guilt that often comes with failure. Don't allow it! A taste of what is to come has been given to you as a reminder that the dream is still alive.

This is the moment when momentum overtakes stagnation. The moment when you can dream again. The moment you are reminded that though you failed and faltered, the dream is still alive—the vision has once again become clear. Enjoy the taste of the promise.

STUCK IN MEDIOCRITY

The second dimension and all that it entails can evoke a sense of defeat that obscures your God-size vision. When that happens, mediocrity ensues.

The book of Genesis highlights a man named Terah—coincidentally, Abraham's father—who experienced mediocrity and never recovered. Terah had a vision. He wanted to reach the land of Canaan. Terah set out with his family from Ur of the Chaldees, as God had promised this land to Abraham and his descendants. However, they reached Haran, and something happened. Genesis 11:31-32 (ESV) tells us that "they went forth together to go from Ur of Chaldees to go into the land of Canaan, but when they came to Haran, they settled there."

How often do we start with a dream or vision and settle along the way? Moments of failure creep in, and we settle. Betrayal unexpectedly pierces our hearts, and we settle. We get tired, face obstacles, or find it convenient to stay where we are. We compromise and convince ourselves that we can only put up with so much—less than what we had dreamed or envisioned. But settling for mediocrity is not part of your God-size dream; it does not fit in with your God-size vision.

The word mediocre literally means "in a middle state." That is, you are not where you used to be, but there is no forward movement either. It is inhabiting the place between failure and success.

The third dimension serves as an exhilarating reminder that the promise is still alive; that the vision has once again become clear. However, it also serves as a cautionary admonition that just as it stands in the middle, between the first and the fifth dimensions, it can also become your mediocre dwelling place.

For Abraham and Sarah, there were many reasons why they should have basked in the enjoyment of Isaac's birth. Why wouldn't they? He represented the beginning of the fulfillment of Abram's (now Abraham) God-size vision. Although Isaac's birth demonstrates God's faithfulness, it was not the full realization of the promise. The vision transcended a single son. So, though its taste overpowered the bitterness of Abraham's failure, he could not accommodate his emotions too much and make the taste a mediocre dwelling place that would never grow into its fulfillment.

JOSEPH'S TASTE

Think about our protagonist Joseph. His God-size dreams have provoked mockery from his brothers. Their mockery has turned to envy and their envy to hatred. The once beloved son of the house has now been sold into slavery. Can you imagine Joseph's overwhelming sea of emotions? Perhaps he asked himself, *What have I done to deserve this? I have gone from one betrayal to another. When is it going to end?* But as I have stated before, no dimension lasts forever.

Joseph's God-size dream superseded the actions of his detractors. His dream, coupled with his character, was a launching pad for the fulfillment of his dream, though his circumstances could have been the beginning of his demise. By an act of providence, Joseph landed a position in the house of an Egyptian officer. So providential was his experience that the Bible points out: "The LORD was with Joseph, so he became a successful man" (Genesis 39:2, NASB).

//

> **No matter the success he experienced, Joseph must distinguish between the FULLNESS of his dream and a TASTE of that fullness.**

////////////

This is where I literally smile as I write this manuscript. As I process the progression of each dimension, I mentally navigate the roller coaster of emotions that comes with each one. My mind revisits the exhilaration that may have come with Joseph receiving not one but two versions of a God-size dream, albeit not without some level of uncertainty. Then, just as he is daydreaming of how the dream would manifest, he finds himself in the hands of betrayers. To exacerbate the situation, his betrayal came at the hands of his own family. Ever felt that way? Just as the overwhelming sting of his brothers' perfidiousness seems never-ending, he finds relief in a taste of success.

Why a taste? Without spoiling it too much for you, I will say that his temporary success was exactly that—temporary. As such, no matter the success he experienced, he must distinguish between the fullness of his dream and a taste of that fullness.

ENJOY THE TASTE

In the fifth dimension part of this book, I will elaborate on how to make a clear distinction between a taste of what is to come and the fullness of a God-size dream or vision. But for now, let me urge you . . . enjoy the taste. Enjoying the taste of what is to come prepares you for a greater dimension. Let me give you a few examples.

> **Do not become so enamored with the taste that you miss the next dimension.**

Whether you are familiar with some of the biblical stories shared throughout this book or not, they follow a progression that closely parallels the fifth-dimension model. So, if you are unfamiliar with Joseph's story, the taste was Potiphar's house, and it prepared him to steward the fulfillment of his dream. So, I wonder, what would have happened if Joseph had fought the process? What would have happened if Joseph had not given the very best of himself even while experiencing some of the worst moments of his life? It is anyone's guess. But I speculate: could he have missed some crucial moments that would have catalyzed fulfillment?

Am I suggesting you disregard those tastes as temporary once you realize they are not the fulfillment of something greater? Not at all! Quite the contrary! I am suggesting you enjoy them as a relief from the second dimension of failure or betrayal. I am suggesting that you savor those moments—however short or long they may be—but do not become so enamored with the taste that you miss the next dimension.

Numerous individuals have had to make a distinction between taste and fulfillment before experiencing the fullness of a God-size dream.

- The people of Israel were instructed to send spies into a land God had promised them. The spies came back with a sample of the fruit of the land; a taste of what they would experience. But at the end of the day, it was only a taste. It did not matter how many grapes, pomegranates, and figs they brought back; they needed reminding that it was only a taste.
- Joseph experienced unprecedented success while serving as a slave in Potiphar's house—he was more like an officer in command than a slave. But when the time came to make a distinction between settling or running toward something greater, he had to remind himself that it was only a taste.
- Abraham finally got to set his eyes on, and hold, his son Isaac. But when the time came to lose himself in the excitement

of Isaac or press forward toward the fulfillment of a greater dream, he had to remind himself that it was only a taste.

- Even Jesus Christ, who came to earth to redeem humanity and save us from living beneath our God-intended purpose by dying for our sins, experienced a taste of heaven on a mountain where He was transfigured. As powerful and divine as that was, it was only a taste. He still had to press forward toward the fulfillment of a God-size dream.

What about you? Have you experienced a taste of something only to become enamored with it and then see it come to an end? Why is that? It is because the dimension of failure or betrayal has dealt such a brutal blow to your emotional stability that to bask in a taste of something great provides relief. Who wouldn't want to settle in moments of relief?

Like the story of my firstborn, who wouldn't want to experience the exhilaration of the birth of your children? After all, it feels like eternal bliss! Should you disregard those moments simply because they won't last forever? No! Quite the contrary. You enjoy every moment—every milestone. Yet, the truth is, those moments must grow and become something greater.

Enjoy the taste that has reminded you that the dream—that vision—is still alive.

When those moments come, you must decide to shift your thinking. You cannot get stuck wondering, worrying, or feeling anxious as if the fulfillment of something has come to an end. No! You must realize that it was a taste that demanded your attention and prepared you for another dimension of your life—a dimension of growth, of maturity, and of preparation for what is to come. And how you handle that taste can very well determine what your future will look like (but more on this in a later chapter).

For now, enjoy the taste that has helped you transcend the season of failure or betrayal. Enjoy the taste that has reminded you that the dream—that vision—is still alive. For now, bask in the taste, and learn to recognize the reminders that help keep the dream alive!

12

ON A DIME

"A taste of what the future holds is God's way of
reminding you to keep the dream alive."
—C. Olmeda

Amid life's trials and tribulations, it is often easy to lose sight of our God-size dreams. We get so caught up in the chaos, so overwhelmed by the challenges we face in the dimension of failure and betrayal that we begin to doubt whether our dreams are even attainable. Yet, in those moments of despair, I believe that God sends reminders—subtle nudges, unexpected blessings, or moments of clarity—to reassure us that there is still a purpose, a plan, and a dream for our lives.

One of the most powerful reminders comes through nature. In the book of Genesis, we read about God's masterful creation of the heavens and the earth. Throughout the Bible, nature is often used as a metaphor for God's love, faithfulness, and creativity. The beauty of a sunrise painting the sky with its bright hues of color, the gentle rustle of leaves in the wind, or the intricate design of a flower can serve as reminders of God's presence and His promise of a hopeful future and fulfillment of dreams.

DREAMS ARE BIRTHED IN CHAOS

This book, coincidentally, was framed during one of the most difficult moments of my life. As I was coming to the end of finalizing a master's degree, one of my professors asked our class cohort to find a remote place and meditate for at least half a day. No other agenda . . . just meditate. He said, "As you do, begin to write whatever you experience." That was it! Those were his instructions.

In agreement, I traveled to a retreat center about one hour away from my home. With no expectations whatsoever, I decided to spend the day out in the woods. I remember it vividly. It was a hot, calm, mid-fall day. No wind, no city noise, and very few people anywhere in sight. The day was perfect for a day of meditation. If you are anything like me, my mind was cluttered with my to-do list, preconceived notions about what this assignment would look like, and a slew of other personal matters. Not surprisingly, it was difficult for me to experience absolute silence. It took a great deal of intentionality to quiet those internal voices.

Again, with no preset agenda, I decided to take a long walk from a private space I had reserved in an adjacent conference center, through the woods, and up a hill to a small chapel. I must admit, everything around me was eerily quiet. I am not sure if all the internal mental noise cluttering my mind was drowning out the sounds of nature, but even the birds didn't seem to chirp—no leaves were rustling, and not one animal or outdoor critter could be seen.

As I trekked my way to the chapel, attempting to be fully present at the moment, I stopped halfway up the dirt path and wondered why and how it could be so quiet on a fall afternoon. Shouldn't I see and hear the leaves move? Before another thought could creep its way into my already crowded thoughts, I could sense the beginning of a rustle. There is no other way to explain it than "surreal." As if nature were speaking, a rustling like something out of the *Chronicles of Narnia* occurred so quickly and so suddenly that it caused me to stop dead in my tracks. One minute, the dead silence was causing me to question what I was missing, and the next moment, nature was speaking in a way that sent chills down my spine.

As only the person experiencing it can articulate it, I heard a voice. The voice reminded me, *I am here!* It was not an audible voice. It was an impression deep within me. A reminder from God, a reminder so clear that it left no doubt in me that the moment I was experiencing was truly divine! I took a moment to bask in what I considered to be a sacred moment. In an instant, I was reminded of a psalm which highlights that "the heavens declare the glory of God; the skies proclaim the work of his hands" (Psalm 19:1, NIV). God had caught my attention through creation, and I was listening!

Instead of continuing my trek toward the chapel, I returned to the room in the conference center. In conjunction with the assignment, I was anxious to write about what I had experienced. As I sat down, pen and pad in hand, instead of writing about what had just occurred, I started to pen the outline for this manuscript as if by divine revelation. I immediately realized that I had God-size dreams embedded deep within me. Yet, moments of failure and betrayal—and all life's challenges—had all but destroyed those dreams. But by God's divine foresight, here I was, reminded that even amid my challenges, God was present and found it fitting to speak to me about greater things to come.

///

To not be fully present is to miss out on the birth of divine dreams.

///////

Pause with me for a moment and think about this. At that moment, nothing had changed, yet everything had changed. Oh, the paradox! Nothing about my personal challenges had changed. Concerns I had about this stage in my life and everything happening around me had not dissipated. I had not purchased a new house, opened a new business, or received an influx of money or anything of grand material significance. Yet, everything had changed. I was divinely reminded that, number one, God was fully present. Secondly, I realized that no temporal personal challenges can stop God-size dreams from embedding deep within me. Thirdly, I learned that to not be fully present is to miss out on the birth of divine dreams. I would never have guessed that dreams could be birthed in the middle of chaos.

Never be afraid to take time off from a hurried life to listen. "What am I listening for?" you may ask. Let me answer that this way. I didn't know what I was listening for when I journeyed off to a retreat center to work on an assignment with very few directions. With a background in spiritual, ministry-based history, I can rattle off some textbook answer that may sound spiritually aligned with some sort of sacred direction. I can give you a textbook answer about how I was listening for the voice of God or seeking to become more spiritually attuned. I could tell you that I was seeking to gain direction and answers to some of the challenges I was enduring. Yet, the truth is, it was none of the above. I was on an assignment to seek peace and quiet and write about my experience. Nothing more, nothing less.

So, sometimes, taking time to listen is not just journeying through a time in meditation with some preconceived notion of what you want to say or do. Sometimes, it is about stepping out in obedience and being fully present in the moment. It is about allowing God to be God in your life.

However they may come, reminders can catalyze an amazing future. Even though those moments may not come with instantaneous changes, they change something within you that ultimately produces the bandwidth and wherewithal to endure. Those moments stir in you the resilience to press forward and accomplish God-size dreams. Don't miss the moment!

TEN IS COMPLETION

That sacred moment kicked off years of reminders. Not just reminders, but much-needed reminders in some of the most vulnerable moments of my life. As my journey through my grad work ensued and persisted into post-graduate work, so did the God-size dreams. Except, like many of us, my current circumstances did not match my God-size dreams.

I have lost count of the numerous numbers of people I have spoken to with God-size dreams and visions whose financial status did not match the magnitude of their dreams. People whose personal circle of influence did not match the level of impact they were created for. People whose resources did not match their level of innovation. Yet, they pressed forward. They did not know when, how, or through whom they would accomplish the dreams embedded within them, yet they pressed forward. Have you found yourself in that conundrum?

When a disequilibrium exists between the magnitude of your dreams and the state of your resources, reminders keep you from aborting those dreams. This is not some made-up conceptualization of how God-size dreams work. No! The reminders are God's way of keeping your dream alive while you navigate each of the dimensions delineated throughout this book. Reminders often show up in the dimension of taste because they become nudges— cues—to keep you moving forward despite uncertainties. They become a taste of sorts, of what is to come.

As time passed and I returned to my ministerial and academic life, something odd began to happen. At first, I thought nothing of it. As the occurrences increased, I knew they were not coincidental. I started finding dimes in the most unusual places.

Now, I will be the first to tell you that I am not a very mystical type of individual. I often tell emerging and very spiritually motivated leaders to do great things, and when they feel like their heads are in the clouds, they better make sure that their feet are planted on the ground. I want to remind them to make certain that they are as practical as they are spiritual.

So, I have never been one to engage too much in biblical numerology, although I believe it has its place. But as the dime-finding phenomenon increased, so did my desire to look deeper into any potential meaning. I found that the number ten is associated with completion. I am not a mathematician, but I do know that ten completes a cycle. The moment you get to ten, anything after is an increase in its repetition. For instance, the number eleven is not a new number, per se. It is ten, increased by one—a number already included in the initial set of ten. Ten, in essence, is the number of completion. The Ten Commandments in the Hebrew Scriptures, for instance, denoted a complete set of mandates forming the framework for moral and God-honoring behavior.

What was I experiencing, and why was I finding dimes everywhere? I wasn't finding pennies, nickels, or quarters. I was finding dimes. The more this phenomenon evolved, the more I noticed that I would find a dime in moments when I needed an ever-so-subtle reminder to keep dreaming and pressing forward. If I was at a decision-making crossroads and my emotions were getting the best of me, I would find a dime. When the magnitude of the dream became so much greater than my resources, I would find a dime. Whether familial, financial, emotional, or relational—if I was going through a moment, like many of us periodically do, when I felt like throwing in the proverbial towel, I would find a dime. For many, "on a dime" can serve as an axiom denoting speed. For me, they were reminders.

Throughout the years, dime-finding became a regular occurrence at just the right moments. So much so that all it took was one moment to solidify and assure me that I was not imagining or conjuring up some mystical phenomenon to be dismissed as coincidence.

One Sunday morning, we had a guest speaker scheduled to deliver the morning sermon at our church. Although I knew him well, we did not have the type of relationship that required us to communicate often. As a matter of fact, we had never spoken of personal matters except for general conversations regarding a national organization we were both part of. Yet, this morning was different.

The minister went about preaching his morning sermon. He proceeded to pray for people who desired prayer. Just before he handed the microphone over, he called me to the altar. Without hesitation, he reached into his pocket and grabbed something in his hand. He looked at me and said, "I normally don't do this, and quite frankly, I do not know exactly what this means, but I have been prompted by God to share something with you." He grabbed my hand and asked me to open it. He looked at me in the eyes and said, "This may mean something to you," as he placed whatever he had in his hand in mine. As I looked into my hand and nearly passed out in shock, he continued, "I felt prompted by God to put ten dimes in your hand and remind you that whatever God begins, He completes!" As tears streamed down my face, he reminded me, "Ten is the number of completion, and God wants to remind you that His dreams over your life will be fulfilled. In moments of despair, keep pressing forward because what you see as incomplete, God already sees as finished!"

///

The more dimes I found, the more my rhetoric changed.

///////////

Talk about a reminder! It doesn't become clearer than that! I knew from that moment on that dimes were God's way of reminding me that if I found myself challenged by the dimension of failure or betrayal, I needed to press forward because the dimension of taste was right around the corner. Dimes became God-winks for me. They became a divine assurance from God, reminding me, "I got you!"

The more dimes I found, the more my rhetoric changed. Initially, I was grateful for the reminders that some of the most difficult seasons of my life would pass. But as the years passed, every time I found a dime at the most unexpected moment or in the most random place, I would smile and say, "Thank you, God, for completion!" The more it happened, the more my prayers of gratitude changed. I would thank God for answering prayers even before I saw them fulfilled.

For instance, one afternoon, with no intention of purchasing a vehicle, I felt an urge to pull into a car dealership on my way from a meeting back to my office. The vehicle I was driving had extremely high mileage and was giving me quite a bit of trouble. As I pulled in, I saw a beautiful black sedan that caught my attention. Interestingly, it was a different make from the dominant cars in that dealership. As the salesman approached, I said, "I would like to take this car for a test drive," as I tapped the top of the car. I opened the door and there on the floor was a dime. Truthfully, I almost purchased it without taking it for a drive, but my practical side won, so I took it for a test drive just to be sure. When I returned, I received one of the best deals and best warranties any dealership has ever offered me. Needless to say, I drove away that afternoon with that vehicle, which turned out to be one of the best vehicles I have ever owned.

Please do not misconstrue my dime-finding story as an answer to your challenges or personal inquiries. Do not make a hasty decision because you found a dime only moments prior. However, I am asking you to be open to reminders. For me, it has been (and continues to be) dimes. For you, it may be something else. Be comforted that God has a way of reminding you to keep the dream alive because you are not meant to go to the grave with an unrealized God-size dream!

13

CAN YOU BE TRUSTED?

"When you are faithful with a taste, you can be trusted to be faithful with abundance!"
—C. Olmeda

What will you do while you wait? What will you do while you navigate through the uncertainties of the dimension of failure or betrayal? What will you do with the realization that what may have looked like fulfillment was only a taste? My recommendation is that you demonstrate your character by being faithful to the opportunities presented before you. Whatever you do, do not draw back in fear and trepidation or succumb to frustration. Do not become stagnant and settle for the status quo. When you recognize that opportunities often come to test your resilience and resolve, your faithfulness will demonstrate that you can be trusted.

In the journey of life, trust is a fundamental cornerstone that shapes our relationships and opportunities. It is a delicate and precious commodity. The concept of being trusted with little and proving yourself worthy of greater trust, even amid adversity, is a timeless principle and precursor to stepping into a greater dimension.

The adage "To whom much is given, much is required" underscores the responsibility that comes with trust. However, before one can be trusted with much, one must first demonstrate he is reliable with little, and it is here that the fifth-dimension journey brings you to a crossroads. Do you sit back and wait for something greater to happen, or do you demonstrate faithfulness and trust in what may seem like insignificant or irrelevant opportunities?

Being trusted with little is an opportunity to showcase integrity, diligence, and commitment. It is the small act of showing up on time, completing tasks to the best of one's ability, and being consistent that lays the foundation for trust. These acts might seem minor, but they are the building blocks of character and competence. They signal to others that one is dependable, attentive to detail, and capable of handling greater responsibilities—a greater assignment.

UNEXPECTED PROMOTIONS

Trust me, I am a witness to this journey of faithfulness and trust, even while navigating seasons of difficulty and uncertainty. Shortly after I had married my now wife of over thirty years, I was tested with being trusted with little, and the dimes were my taste that promised better days ahead.

I remember it all too well. I was a newlywed who had moved from my home state to my wife's home state. With the move came several turns of events that left me struggling to gain my financial footing. What was I going to do? I was a new husband and had a household and wife to look after and take care of. I had God-size dreams, yet my current condition did not match my dreams. Do I sit and wait? Do I become angry at God for my challenges? Or do I press forward and do whatever I can while I pray for better days?

I wish I could tell you that I had a plan. I didn't! I was in survival mode. I felt like Joseph—betrayed by his brothers, sold as a slave, and assigned to Potiphar's house as a servant. I was in survival mode, doing the very best I could with the opportunities before me.

In addition to a full-time job, I secured a part-time job at a telephone marketing company in an attempt to get ahead. You probably know them all too well—the people who randomly call you at odd hours to sell you insurance, credit cards, and a plethora of other merchandise. That was me.

So, despite the dreams embedded within me, this season would require my wife to drop me off at my morning job and proceed to her own job. Then, she would have to pick me up after work and drive me to my part-time job. As if that were not enough, she would have to pick me up past 10 p.m. at night to do it all over again the next day. Unquestionably, that schedule began to take a toll on our new marriage within a short period of time.

If I did what others did not do, I could potentially get what others did not get.

Despite that hardship, I had been taught growing up that you should give your very best and put your proverbial best foot forward despite life's challenges. With this in mind, I would either stop at home for a quick change of clothes or pack a set of my *Sunday bests* before going to my part-time job. If you knew how people dressed at this telemarketing firm, you would find dressing up just to sit down in front of a telephone in a room of about one hundred people and making phone calls for four or five hours to be an exercise in futility. Yet, even with the part-time status and despite the journey through a difficult season, I walked in every evening and worked like my life depended on it. Like the president of a company and to the mockery of some coworkers, I would often walk in with a suit and tie.

I cannot emphasize how many times I had to convince myself that I was not being ridiculous. I repeatedly talked myself out of dubbing myself a fool for thinking that, somehow, being different would set me apart from the many employees who often walked in like they had just rolled out of bed. Yet, despite the internal battles, mockery, and what seemed like a dead-end life, I convinced myself that if I did what others did not do, I could potentially get what others did not get.

About two months into the job, I was summoned into the executive director's office for a meeting. With a rapid heart growing faster by the second, I wondered what I had done to get in trouble. *Maybe the quality control representative who listened in on our calls reported me to the director,* I thought. As if my heart was not already beating faster than it would after a high-intensity training exercise, the executive director told me that the reason for our meeting was to let me know that in two days, the senior vice president would travel to our office and desired to meet with the both of us.

I was familiar with the senior vice president. His visits were never good. I had witnessed him get into a screaming match with one of the supervisors. Trust me, I wanted no part in meeting with him. Despite my inquiries, the executive director refused to warn me about why this corporate officer would want to meet with me. Admittedly, it felt like the longest two days of my life.

Two days later, in the *Sunday best* I had grown accustomed to working in, I stepped into the executive director's office for the much-anticipated meeting. "Charles," she said sternly, "you may find this meeting a surprise. But he (the senior vice president) asked to meet with you based on multiple conversations we have had about you."

At that point, I wanted to interrupt our conversation and say, "Just tell me what I did wrong, and let's expedite this process."

///

We have all experienced that nagging feeling of discontent, and it should make us uncomfortable enough to press forward until something changes.

///////////

As I anxiously awaited bad news, the senior vice president interrupted the conversation and announced that the executive director had accepted a position at another company, and he wanted to consider me for the now vacant position. Was I hearing him correctly? And how do you hide the biggest smile you have ever smiled without looking unprofessional? I couldn't believe it. *I just got here a couple of months ago,* I thought! *Some supervisors have been here for years! What about them?* The thoughts kept coming. *I have never managed this many people! My knowledge is limited!* On and on, all sorts of questions and concerns flooded my mind. But without hesitation, I said, "Thank you! I would be honored to be considered for the position!"

Over the next couple of months, I lost 50 percent of my supervisors who were angry that an over-dressed, young, and inexperienced individual had been promoted to the top position at that facility. All I needed was a taste—a taste of promotion, leadership potential, and unexpected opportunities. I chose to fight the complacency that often comes when we get a taste, and instead, I pressed on.

What are you dissatisfied with? That will be different for you than it was for me. We have all experienced that nagging feeling of discontent, and it should make us uncomfortable enough to press forward until something changes.

What had been an insignificant part-time job to make ends meet would now replace my full-time job and increase my income more than both jobs combined. Being the God-fearing, God-size dreamer I was, I could feel my emotions swell up in gratitude. *It was worth the mockery,* I thought one day. *Thank you, God, for the ability to stand out and give my very best despite the current chaos,* I prayed.

Difficult times are often the crucibles that test whether you can be trusted.

As the thoughts of gratitude flooded my mind, so did the thoughts of *what if?* What if I would have blended in like everyone else? What if I would have called in "sick" whenever I felt tired or frustrated from living on the proverbial hamster wheel, running in circles day in and day out? What if I treated this like a second job and simply attempted to get by without giving it my very best?

Let me remind you that difficult times are often the crucibles that test whether you can be trusted. Adversity has a way of revealing true character. It strips away the façade and exposes the core of who we are. When faced with little challenges God has entrusted to us, whether personal or professional, how we act speaks volumes. It is easy to be trustworthy when circumstances are favorable, but the real test comes when the pressure mounts, resources are scarce, and the path forward is shrouded in uncertainty.

Being trusted with little during such times requires resilience. It demands an inner strength to persevere, to maintain one's standards of excellence, and to keep one's word. It is about being resourceful. It is about finding solutions within constrained circumstances and maintaining a positive attitude even when the odds are stacked against you. Such resilience not only helps one navigate through tough times but also demonstrates to others that your trustworthiness is not contingent on circumstances.

As you prove your fortitude—your moral fiber—in the face of adversity, you earn the trust of those around you. How do you think our protagonist, Joseph, transitioned from serving as a slave to receiving the full trust of his master over his entire household and possessions? Joseph's character was associated with reliability and strength, and so could yours be.

//

Pay attention to who God puts in your life and listen.

////////

An integral reputation built over time through consistent actions opens doors to greater opportunities. Leaders and decision-makers tend to take notice of those who can be counted on, especially when it is difficult to do so. They recognize the value and potential of those who do not falter when trusted with little, and subsequently, those leaders will trust them with more.

As you remain faithful and prove you can be trusted, God will often place people in your path to propel you closer and closer to the fulfillment of your God-size dreams. So, pay attention to who God puts in your life and listen. This is why you should never burn bridges or sabotage relationships. Honor and respect relationships, first, because people matter, and second, because they may be door openers to your next promotion.

The next couple of years were fruitful in more ways than I could have ever imagined. The quality control representative whom I thought was there to give me a scathing review was a conduit to yet another promotion. She suggested that my professionalism and attire would fit better within the banking industry. As such, she served as a bridge that launched me into banking management for quite a number of years. Coincidentally, in God's omniscience, this season became part of the framework for many of the decisions I have since had to make to secure ministry properties and oversee building projects.

///

Trustworthiness is not just about what one does when everyone is watching but when no one is looking.

//////////

The transition from being trusted with little to being trusted with more is not just about increased responsibilities or the scale of tasks. It is about the depth of earned trust. Deeper trust allows for significant opportunities to influence, lead, and make a difference. It measures one's ability to handle complexity, manage risks, and inspire others.

Moreover, being trusted with greater things is not the end goal; it is a new beginning. It is a chance to continue the cycle of trust, to mentor others in the art of reliability, and to contribute to a culture where trust is valued and nurtured. It is an invitation to set an example for others. It is a chance to show that trustworthiness is not just about what one does when everyone is watching but when no one is looking.

Stepping out to distinguish yourself from others becomes a testament to your character and a predictor of future success. Through trials and tribulations, those who remain steadfast in their commitment to trustworthiness not only survive but thrive. Like those who have traveled a similar journey and have overcome, you, too, can become a pillar upon which greater things are built. Your journey ultimately becomes a beacon of hope and inspiration for others to follow. Trust, therefore, is not just a measure of your current standing but a bridge to a future filled with possibilities, including the fulfillment of your God-size dreams. It is a journey worth embarking on, a challenge worth accepting, and a legacy worth leaving behind.

14

DON'T SETTLE

"Don't settle for second-best, when greatness is at your fingertips."
—C. Olmeda

*"Don't let anyone make you feel like second-best. Know
your worth and refuse to settle for anything less."*
—Author Unknown

Settling for second-best is a concept that subtly and often creeps into our lives, convincing us that what we have is good enough. It attempts to convince us that striving for more is unnecessary or even a sign of being ungrateful. However, this mindset can be a significant barrier to realizing the full potential of our God-size dreams. These dreams are not just lofty aspirations; they are visions that align with our destiny and the purpose we are meant to fulfill in our lifetime. Settling for second-best may seem like a pragmatic approach in the short term, but it ultimately blinds us to the fullness of what we could achieve. The challenge is that second-best often comes disguised in very attractive ways.

GREENER ISN'T ALWAYS BETTER

Abraham and his nephew Lot can attest to that challenge all too well. Within the scope of biblical history, the story of Lot stands as a cautionary tale about the perils of being seduced by surface appearances and settling for what, at a glance, seems to be the best option. Lot's decision to choose the lush plains of Jordan near the city of Sodom over the more challenging lands left a profound impact on his life. It serves as a lesson on the importance of discernment and foresight.

Lot's story begins with a dispute between his herdsmen and those of his uncle Abraham as they travel together. To resolve the conflict, Abraham proposes that they separate, and he gives Lot the first choice of the land. Lot lifts his eyes and sees the whole plain of Jordan. Every corner of it was well-watered "like the garden of the LORD, like the land of Egypt" (Genesis 13:10, NKJV). This verdant vista, reminiscent of paradise itself, captivated Lot. The beauty and apparent prosperity of the land blinded him to any potential pitfalls. He chose what he perceived as the best, not realizing it was only second-best in the grand scheme of his destiny.

Lot's choice was based on immediate appearance, without consideration for the moral and spiritual climate of the cities that dotted the plains: Sodom and Gomorrah. His decision to dwell near Sodom eventually led to assimilation into a society marked by depravity and sin. The green pastures that promised so much delivered a life fraught with challenges and spiritual decay. Lot's superficial choice cost him the deeper, more meaningful blessings that come from walking in alignment with God's will.

As time passed, the consequences of Lot's decision became increasingly evident. The wickedness of Sodom and Gomorrah provoked the wrath of God, leading to their ultimate destruction. Lot, who once sat at the gates of Sodom, a position of honor and influence, found himself fleeing for his life, instructed not to look back at the burning cities. His wife, unable to resist the pull of what they were leaving behind, turned into a pillar of salt. Lot's choice to settle for the appealing green pastures resulted in the loss of his home, his wife, and his standing.

GUILTY

I am just as guilty as many of you may be. Many times in life, we become enamored by the attractive and often seductive tugging of trends, a more lucrative business, a more fun-filled environment, or a more popular crowd, only to live on the fringes of destruction. We underestimate the power of evil forces that attempt to detract us from fulfilling God-size dreams.

Like Lot, we may feel like we have the self-discipline to get close enough to the proverbial Sodom and Gomorrah without engaging in compromising or destructive behaviors. Yet, we underestimate the power our choices may have over our spouses, children, and familial connections. Like Lot and his wife, you may be able to escape the damaging effects of playing with fire but may do so at the expense of losing loved ones.

LESSONS LEARNED

Lot's experience teaches us that choices based solely on external allure can lead to dire consequences. It reminds us that what may seem like the best option can be deceptive. It reminds us that the true best choice is often one that aligns with divine principles and long-term spiritual well-being. The green pastures may offer temporary satisfaction, but they cannot compare to the fulfillment of living out God-size dreams.

Despite the tragedy that befell Lot, his story also offers a glimmer of hope and redemption. His daughters, though products of a compromised society, were spared destruction. This serves as a reminder that even when we make poor choices, God's grace can still bring forth good from the situation. It is never too late to realign yourself with the God-size dreams and visions embedded within you and seek their fulfillment. So, look beyond the surface and consider the long-term implications of your choices. You may avoid the pitfalls of settling for second-best and instead pursue the God-size dreams that lead to true and lasting fulfillment.

COMPLACENCY

Second-best also comes disguised as complacency. Complacency is the silent thief that robs us of our potential. It breeds a sense of dissatisfaction and regret as we realize that we have not lived up to our full potential.

Orpah's decision speaks to this all-too-popular decision-making process. Orpah is the daughter-in-law of Naomi within the familial narrative of the book of Ruth. The story unfolds when Elimelech, a man from Bethlehem of Judah, along with his wife, Naomi, and their two sons, Mahlon and Kilion, are forced to flee their home due to a famine. We may presume that Naomi was comforted, knowing both of her sons were married. But then, a series of unfortunate events led to the death of Naomi's husband, Elimelech, and her two sons:

*When Naomi heard that the L*ORD *had come to the aid of his people [in Bethlehem] by providing food for them, she and her daughters-in-law prepared to return home from there. With her two daughters-in-law she left the place where she had been living and set out on the road that would take them back to the land of Judah.*
—*Ruth 1:6-7 (NIV)*

Perhaps, Naomi felt guilty about taking her daughters-in-law away from their land and along with her back to Judah. As such, she attempted to convince them to go back to their mothers' homes.

//

> ### Settling often occurs when we prioritize immediate comfort over long-term fulfillment.

/////////

Why not go back? Moab is their home. It is what they have known all their lives. To make matters worse, the men they have married are now deceased. So, why not find comfort in what is familiar? To that end, Orpah agreed with Naomi, kissed her goodbye, and returned to her home. She returned to what was familiar. Ruth, however, thought differently. Ruth clung to Naomi and refused to return to the status quo. We don't fully know why, but from the text, we get the sense that Ruth sensed something powerful about the God Naomi professed. She begged Naomi not to force her to leave and return to Judah. When Naomi saw her persistence to stay, she yielded to her request.

Settling often occurs when we prioritize immediate comfort over long-term fulfillment. It is the path of least resistance, offering a quick fix to the challenges we face. However, this approach is shortsighted, and it may have very well been for Orpah. Immediate gratification disregards the inner voice that calls us to pursue a greater purpose. God-size dreams require patience and perseverance, qualities that settling undermines.

Ruth's vision for something different, albeit unknown at the time, paid off. Her love and compassion for Naomi, resilience, and work ethic helped secure her provision and promotion. Ruth ultimately married one of the wealthiest men in Bethlehem and gave birth to a son whom Naomi took under her care. Subsequently, Ruth's vision for something more and her refusal to remain complacent became the "restorer of life and a nourisher of [Naomi's] old age" (Ruth 4:15, NKJV). What's more, her son, whom she named Obed, became the father of Jesse, who became the father of David—one of the greatest kings in biblical history.

After observing Ruth's journey and decision-making ability, what may have been the best option for Orpah now seemed like second-best in light of Ruth's success. Often, acquiescing to comfort becomes the enemy of a greater tomorrow, causing us to settle into complacency. I wonder how many dreams have gone unfilled, new territories undiscovered, relationships never materialized, and vicious cycles never broken because people chose to revert to a place of complacency and familiarity rather than take steps of faith and believe for the fulfillment of God-size dreams.

Some may disagree with me and suggest that Orpah chose a place of contentment. Is not true contentment a state of peace and satisfaction with one's life? However, when we settle for less than we are capable of, we confuse resignation with contentment. So, considering all that Naomi, Ruth, and Orpah had been through, Orpah may have been simply acquiescing to a substandard way of living or returning to a place where she could potentially find peace. The realization that we have not honored potential dreams for a greater tomorrow eventually shatters this fragile, false sense of peace.

Faith is the antidote to the settling mindset.

Let us not forget what this section is about overall. It is about the dimension of taste. A taste of what the future holds can propel some to make the necessary changes to keep the dream alive. For others, when things go awry, they return to a place of conformity, give up, and settle for the status quo.

FAITH

God-size dreams are fueled by vision—a clear and compelling picture of what could be. This vision inspires action and propels us forward. Without it, we are prone to settle. We lose sight of the greater narrative we are called to participate in. Vision requires faith. It requires belief in things not yet seen but hoped for.

Faith is the antidote to the settling mindset. Perhaps in the midst of Ruth's most difficult moment in life, she had faith. Faith in a better life than what she had experienced. Faith in Naomi's God. Faith empowers us to believe in the possibility of achieving something we have never achieved before. Faith gives us the strength to take risks and the resilience to persevere through setbacks. It is the foundation on which the fulfillment of our dreams is built.

As we follow Ruth's journey into a new territory, we find that it became a journey of self-discovery. Her resilient and bold move to provide for herself and Naomi, coupled with her newfound fearlessness to approach the man who would later become her husband, speaks volumes of self-discovery.

So, pursuing God-size dreams is, too, a journey of self-discovery. It reveals our strengths and exposes our weaknesses. Settling for second-best denies us the opportunity to learn and grow. It prevents us from becoming the person we were meant to be—fully alive and engaged in the pursuit of God-size dreams.

Ultimately, God-size dreams align with our divine purpose. They are the expression of our unique role in the grand scheme of life. Settling for second-best is a rejection of this purpose. It is only by embracing and pursuing our God-size dreams that we can experience the fullness of life and the joy of fulfilling our destiny.

What have you settled for? Like Naomi, Ruth, and Orpah, has life been difficult? Do you feel like retreating to a place of peace and comfort for relief? Let me admonish you! Don't settle! Life's difficulties, unexpected turns of events, and even tragedies often become opportunities in disguise. They became a crossroads where your faith can arise to dream beyond what you have been accustomed to. So, dare to dream! Dare to dream beyond the familiar! Move beyond complacency and into the fulfillment of God-size dreams.

15

UNCOMFORTABLE PLACES

"Don't settle for a taste when fulfillment awaits!"
—C. Olmeda

We are coming to the end of the dimension of taste. By now, you should have sensed that although a taste of what is to come may satisfy you for a time, it cannot last forever. I did not say, "It will not last forever!" It can if you let it, at which point it becomes complacency. You do not possess God-size dreams to settle in complacency. The dimension of taste served only as a relief and a reminder. It served as a relief from the difficult dimension of failure or betrayal. It served as a reminder of what awaits. The fulfillment of God-size dreams—God-size vision—awaits.

Our protagonist, Joseph is a great example of the distinction between taste and fulfillment. If you have followed Joseph's trajectory, you may have noticed that his dreams were no ordinary reveries. They were vivid, prophetic glimpses of his future. Imagine the excitement and anticipation that surged within him only to

165

turn into fear and trepidation within a short period of time. Joseph quickly realized that dreams alone do not guarantee fulfillment. They merely provide a taste of what could be. The journey through multiple dimensions provides a clearer picture and, ultimately, assurance of the fulfillment of God-size dreams.

We have already captured a glimpse of Joseph as a slave in an Egyptian officer's (Potiphar's) home. Within the magnificent splendor of this opulent household, Joseph tasted success. Was it the fulfillment of his dream? No! This level of success was not the pinnacle of his dream; it was only a tantalizing morsel. Joseph had to realize that his purpose extended beyond material prosperity.

Subsequently, Potiphar's wife, drawn to Joseph's handsomeness, propositioned him. Her advances attempted to lure him into having sexual relations with her. As Potiphar's wife, she offered more than physical pleasure. She offered a shortcut to comfort and security. Yet, Joseph understood that settling for her advances would compromise his destiny. He could not trade a God-size dream with fleeting satisfaction.

Joseph's response to Potiphar's wife revealed his unwavering commitment to purpose. Joseph fled. He fled because he considered any act of submission to such an immoral act would be considered a great sin against God and a blatant betrayal of his master. He chose to run from temptation rather than settle for momentary pleasure.

We are not meant to live with a sample of a dream. Dreams are meant to be lived. Joseph ran from Potiphar's house, not because he lacked desire. As a young man fueled by normal emotions, I am sure there was a physical or emotional draw to the woman's advances. Yet, he understood that settling would rob him of his destiny. He somehow knew that his God-size dream was meant to be lived, not just sampled.

Joseph's actions remind us that regardless of how successful, how glamorous, or how enticing some things may look, we must sacrifice them and consider them as simply a taste if they put the fulfillment of our God-size dreams in jeopardy. Potiphar's house offered a taste of success, but Joseph knew it wasn't enough. When faced with a moral dilemma, he knew that the initial palace was only a taste. It was a taste of something greater. He had to choose purpose over convenience—commitment to the fulfillment of a dream over complacency.

SACRIFICE THE PROMISE

Our protagonist, Abraham fits the same model. Can you imagine how exhilarated he must have been at the birth of his son Isaac? Just when he thought he would die without a direct heir, Abraham received a God-size vision. He received a vision that superseded the stars of the sky and the sand on the seashore. Despite all his wealth, he was still lacking something. In his case, it was his progeny. So, imagine how proud of and protective he may have been over such a surreal promise. Yet, while Isaac was still very young, the Bible shows us that God tested Abraham.

I am not sure about you, but I don't necessarily look forward to those periods of testing in my life. Those moments when you question life's challenges. When you feel like the glory you were basking in moments earlier has abruptly ended.

I wonder how Abraham felt when he went from embracing his time with Isaac to receiving a directive from God. I could imagine Abraham saying, "Wait, God, what did you say?" when he heard God's command:

> [Yes], take now your son, your only son [of promise], whom you love, Isaac, and go to the region of Moriah, and offer him there as a burnt offering on one of the mountains of which I shall tell you. —Genesis 22:2 (AMP)

Apparently, the urgency and specificity of the matter were part of the instruction. The word "now" certainly signifies urgency or immediacy. And the verb "love" undoubtedly speaks of Abraham's affection toward his son. This was not casual. The instructions were not easy. Yet, at that very moment, Abraham had a decision to make. His decision is not embedded in the immediate instructions as it is in the recollection of his initial God-size vision. Had he been promised a son, or had he been promised countless descendants? Was he going to trust God for the fulfillment of His promise, or was he going to hoard Isaac as a taste?

My purpose here is to draw the parallel between taste and fulfillment, not to express any theological argument about human sacrifice (which, subsequently, God did not allow) or familial abuse in any way, shape, or form. Contextually, and what is considered exegetically, we must differentiate between the cultural and historical context of the text and a New Testament understanding of a sacrifice.

So, as we parse Abraham's conundrum, we realize he had a very difficult choice to make. Does he decide based on his present circumstance, or does he decide on the basis of the initial vision? From the text, we are privy to his decision-making *and* the process of his decision-making.

Abraham decided to follow God's instruction with precision. On their way to make *the sacrifice,* we hear the following:

> Isaac asked, *"Look, the fire and the wood, but where is the lamb for the burnt offering?"* ... Abraham said, *"My son, God will provide for Himself the lamb for a burnt offering."* —Genesis 22:7-8 (AMP)

At that moment, Abraham immediately recognized and acknowledged that because the vision he had for the future was a God-size vision and, therefore, of a divine origin, whatever decision he had to make in alignment with that vision was God's problem, not his. The God who gave the initial vision was the same God who would bring that child back to life if that is what the sacrifice called for. The God who gave him the initial vision would be the same God who would miraculously provide the sacrifice.

That moment was the defining moment for Abraham. That uncomfortable place of decision-making set the pace for the rest of Abraham's life. At that moment, God knew He could trust Abraham with a God-size vision. At that moment, God knew that despite how uncomfortable the situation was for Abraham and his son, he would not become so enamored with the taste that he would be unwilling to risk it all. Abraham was willing to risk it all in obedience because, ultimately, Isaac was not the entire promise; instead, he was a taste and a conduit through which Abraham's God-size vision would be fulfilled.

KNOW THE DIFFERENCE

As you navigate the complex yet necessary challenges of distinguishing between taste and fulfillment, let me provide you with three critical principles that will help you make the distinction: the principle of divine intentionality, the principle of moral engagement, and the principle of ownership.

Principle of Divine Intentionality

As I think through this principle, I recall several challenges with one of my two daughters as a toddler. It has been more than twenty years, yet I still vividly remember the fiasco.

"What is going on over there?" I exclaimed as I heard some bickering and crying coming from a couple of toddlers just one room over. I had stepped out of the room for a brief moment when the bickering ensued. As I walked back into the room, two toddlers were practically ripping a toy apart. As the visiting toddler was hysterically crying and losing her grip on the toy she wanted to play with, my daughter was shouting, "IT'S MINE! IT'S MINE!" Talk about a moment for a parenting lesson!

First, I had to teach my daughter that sharing was caring. Secondly, I had to teach her that the toy could either bring joy to her alone, or she could use it to bring joy to both her and others. Thirdly, she needed to know that her display of ownership was not conducive to relationship-building. Lastly, I had to remind her that the only reason she had that toy was because I had given it to her as a gift.

//

The purpose of Abraham's blessing extended beyond material wealth. It was meant to cascade into generational and global impact.

////////////

Divine intentionality is the principle of understanding why you were given a God-size dream—a God-size vision—to begin with. Remember Abraham? He was extremely wealthy prior to receiving a God-size vision. Yes, perhaps his wealth may have placed his household in a great position for years to come. However, he did not have an heir on whom to pass his inheritance. Further, as the divine vision unfolds, we are let in on a little secret. The purpose of Abraham's blessing extended beyond material wealth. It was meant to cascade into generational and global impact.

How about Joseph? Potiphar's initial trust in him undoubtedly blessed him beyond the status of a slave. Did you get that? The promotion blessed him! Once we are made privy to the fulfillment of Joseph's dreams, we realize that the fulfillment of his God-size dream was intended to impact and save a nation from economic devastation.

Personal dreams and personal accomplishments tend to have limited impact. The fulfillment of God-size dreams and God-size visions carries a much broader impact.

As a young man, I dreamed big. The moment I got a taste of the banking industry and finances, I thought I would become some Wall Street guru making millions of dollars and living the *good life*. Yet, as I matured and submitted my will to the principle of divine intentionality, I surrendered my life to how God wanted to use me to impact others beyond my limited scope of influence. I understood that God's intentions for my life transcended a *personal* blessing.

As I reflect on the sacrifices I have made by running from the proverbial and temporal Potiphars' houses because they didn't align with my God-size dreams, I am grateful that I did not settle for what could have been simply a taste. I never became a Wall Street guru, but I am living a great life serving as a mentor, a leader, and a voice of influence to all those I come in contact with—especially the next generation of leaders.

There is a woman by the name of Hannah in the Bible who suffered and wept constantly because she could not have children. Her nemesis, Peninnah—Hannah's husband's other wife—severely provoked her because of her inability to conceive. (Don't get any ideas, gentlemen. One wife is all you need. This is Old Testament theology. Let's keep it in context . . . humor intended. I digress.) Despite how badly she wanted a child, she prayed that if God would bless her with a male child, she would give him up to the service of God.

God heard her prayer. She could have changed her mind. She could have become so enamored with her new miracle, Samuel, and forgotten about her promise. She didn't. She held to her promise because she knew that the God-size dream that would be birthed through her was intended for a greater purpose than just a personal, familial blessing. As such, Samuel became one of the greatest voices in a time when "the word of the LORD [God] was rare" (1 Samuel 3:1, NIV). Imagine the long-term satisfaction Hannah felt as she witnessed the impact her son made on the lives of people across multiple generations. She submitted to the principle of divine intentionality and was rewarded for it!

Why did Abraham succumb to the call to sacrifice his son Isaac? He understood that his God-size vision was not simply connected to the laughter and cries of a child filling his home but to the generational promotion of blessings.

Could it be that the fulfillment of God-size dreams and God-size visions is not necessarily a divine way of creating impact *for you* as much as it is a divine way to create impact *through you*? Who can you impact by the size and fulfillment of your dream? Who can you influence by the size and impact of your vision?

Principle of Moral Engagement

Why did Joseph run from Potiphar's house, leaving his robe, his position, and his possessions behind? Could it be that his desire for moral engagement spoke more of his character than his position or possessions?

The opposite version of moral engagement is moral disengagement. Drawing on his agentic theory, Dr. Albert Bandura, the Canadian-born American psychologist and originator of social cognitive theory, provides a definitive exposition of the psychosocial mechanism by which people selectively disengage their moral self-sanctions from their harmful conduct. He has suggested that people from all walks of life have the propensity to behave harmfully and still maintain positive self-regard and live in peace with themselves. This is where people justify bad behavior, entitlement, promotions at the expense of others, and so many other actions.[3] Such actions demonstrate moral disengagement.

Conversely, moral engagement suggests that people follow a commitment to positive social interactions and thoughtful care for others. It is the Golden Rule—do unto others as you would have them do unto you (Matthew 7:12). Along this vein, when the God-size dream becomes greater than personal satisfaction, the principle of moral engagement propels you to make decisions that fuel a greater good.

A biblical narrative of a man named Zacchaeus speaks to the shift between moral disengagement and moral engagement.

---

3 Albert Bandura, Moral Disengagement: How People Do Harm and Live with Themselves (New York, NY: Macmillan, 2016).

Zacchaeus was a height-challenged man who climbed a tree to get a glimpse of the much-spoken-about Jesus. His effort did not go unnoticed. As Jesus passed by, He noticed Zacchaeus, called him out by name, and proceeded to invite Himself to the house of this highly despised individual.

Zacchaeus was despised amongst his own Jewish people because he was a tax collector working for the Roman government. Tax collectors were known to force people to pay more money than they owed. Zacchaeus was no different. Yet, the moment he allowed Jesus into his home, he must have received a God-size vision greater than anything he had ever experienced, so much so that the morally disengaged individual's heart was moved to change. Zacchaeus promised to give half his belongings to the poor and pay back four times as much to anyone he had cheated (Luke 19:1-10).

How about you? Have you ever compromised your integrity for personal gain? Have you disregarded the interest of others for personal satisfaction? I have! Like Zacchaeus, I had to confront my own moral disengagement and admit that if I was going to see the fulfillment of God-size dreams, then my actions had to align with something greater than myself! I had to decide to live by the principle of moral engagement if I intended to impact people for generations to come!

Joseph also applied this principle and was rewarded accordingly! The fulfillment of his God-size dream was exceedingly greater than the position and possessions he left in Potiphar's house.

Principle of Ownership

During a recent leadership seminar, my dear friend Chris Sonksen shared a humorous story about his very young granddaughter. He had taken her to a ball game and asked her what kind of snacks she wanted. She chose the familiar and colorful Skittles. Sometime into the game, he leaned over and asked her for some Skittles.

To his surprise, she turned down his request and said, "No, they're mine!"

"It took everything in me not to snatch the bag of Skittles from her hand," he admitted. He retorted with three things: "Did you forget who bought those for you?" "Do you see how big I am compared to you? I have the power and the strength to take them from you with very little effort!" and "I have enough resources that if you ran out, I could get you many more bags of Skittles!"

How many of us hoard things we have received and forget those same three principles Chris shared with his granddaughter? Our protagonist Abraham did not have a problem giving up Isaac because he knew that Isaac was a by-product of divine provision. He knew that the God-size vision he had received extended beyond a single son. It encompassed generations.

There is a narrative about a rich man who had accumulated an enormous amount of resources. The grounds he owned had yielded an abundant harvest. Such was his increase that he didn't know where to store his surplus. So, he said:

I will tear down my barns and build bigger ones, and there I will store my surplus grain. And I'll say to myself, 'You have plenty of grain laid for many years. Take life easy; eat, drink and be merry.' —Luke 12:18-19 (NIV)

Apparently, for this man, life was about himself and his accumulation of wealth. The next verse (v. 20) helps us understand God's perception of the man's building plan because He said, "You fool! This very night your life will be demanded from you. Then who will get what you have prepared for yourself?"

Within this principle of ownership lies the success of our protagonist, Joseph. Running from Potiphar's house proved that nothing he had been given was his. Therefore, to preserve his character, he was willing to walk away from it all. Later in life, he once again experienced unprecedented success. Like before, he knew that the ownership did not belong to him. He was simply a steward—an administrator—of resources.

> ## We can either hoard our resources or allow them to flow through us for greater impact.

Everything we have is because we have been given the breath of life, energy, opportunities, connections, and bandwidth to succeed. You may be tempted to say, "But *I* accomplished this or that!" or "It is *my* effort that has enabled me to be where I am!" The truth is that no success is possible without the breath of life given to us by our Creator. If we learn anything from the stories I have shared, let it be that we can either hoard our resources or allow them to flow through us for greater impact. We can constrain our dreams by limiting them to *our* ownership, or we can admit that resources for God-size dreams are unlimited and can be channeled *through* us to create a greater and more meaningful impact. To do so, you must learn to hold on to things loosely and be open to experiencing the fourth dimension.

4TH DIMENSION
OBEDIENCE

OBEDIENCE

TASTE

FAILURE
OR
BETRAYAL

DREAMS
&
VISIONS

16

FINISH WHAT YOU'VE STARTED

"Commitment is finishing what you've started even when you don't feel like doing it anymore!"
—Author Unknown

By now, you should have realized that settling for a taste is not an option. How, then, do we move forward toward realizing our God-size dreams? The answer is obedience! Obedience is not always easy. God-size dreams often involve challenges, obstacles, and waiting. When those moments arrive, we must decide whether we are going to obey what is necessary to move forward or remain complacent. Why obedience? The first question we must ask before providing a rapid response is, "Where did the God-size dream originate?" Where did the God-size vision come from? Ultimately, the *where* is connected to the *whom*. Who caused such dreams and visions to be embedded deep within your soul? Whether you are a deeply religious, faith-filled person or not, if you are going to address God-size dreams and visions, then you must admit that they transcend your limited abilities.

Therefore, if we recognize that what we are called to accomplish transcends our personal limitations and, therefore, requires God's divine intervention, then we must also deduce that our actions must go beyond personal levels of comfort. That is where obedience becomes necessary. It requires aligning our will with God's will. It requires making decisions that align with the God-size dreams— the God-size visions—that have been given to us. It is when we surrender to an authority greater than ourselves and base our actions on God's divine guidance that we begin to experience the fullness and fulfillment of those dreams and visions.

Have you noticed the emerging process toward fulfillment? It is like a roller-coaster ride. Like Abraham, you are pulled out of your comfort zone and given a vision that is greater than anything you have ever experienced. Like Joseph, one moment, you are coasting through life, and the next moment, you are receiving a dream that shakes you to your core. When those God-size moments arrive, the next thing you expect is some level of progression toward the realization of the vision or dream. Instead, you are met with failure or betrayal.

Just when you think you have had enough and that the season of failure or betrayal has taken a toll on your life, you experience a taste of the fulfillment of the initial vision or dream. That dimension comes in like a breath of fresh air. You can breathe again. Like Abraham, you have overcome your failure with Hagar and can enjoy looking into the eyes of Isaac. Like Joseph, you have endured the betrayal of those closest to you and can now breathe while basking in the grandeur of a palatial experience. Finally, a taste of the fulfillment of your God-size dream. Finally, a taste of the fulfillment of your God-size vision.

I wish life were that simple. Except, like Abraham, just when you are beginning to enjoy your time with your perceived promise, you are asked to sacrifice him. Like Joseph, just when you feel you have planted your footing in a stable and exceptional environment, you find yourself leaving it all behind to preserve your character.

All of it may seem unfair. At first glance, it seems like a cruel joke. "When will I ever see the fulfillment of my God-size vision?" you may ask. "When will I see the fullness of my God-size dream?" The instability of the process may seem unfair, but let me let you in on a little secret: it is necessary. Every dimension is a dimension closer to the fulfillment of the grandeur embedded within your very soul.

The question is, do you have the resilience and focus to finish what you started? Like Abraham, do you have the resilience and faith to heed the directives to sacrifice the very thing you love? Can you and will you obey that prompting? Like Joseph, will you continue to preserve your character and integrity despite having been betrayed and lied about with no way to prove yourself? Will you finish what you have started despite setbacks and opposition?

When we navigate these tumultuous waters of failure or betrayal, it can feel like things will never get better. Joseph did not have the hindsight we have and numerous examples of how we know that things *will* get better. They have to if we are to witness the fullness of the fifth dimension.

DERAILMENT

Many of us do not finish things we have started. Not because we do not desire to do so, but because interruptions derail us. Beginning the journey well is often not the problem. Remaining consistent when confronted with many other challenges is usually what makes finishing strong so difficult.

Imagine this scenario. I set out to clean my garage. Not even ten minutes have passed, and I find a tool that belongs to my neighbor. Tool in hand, I think, *What better time than now to return it?* On my way out of the garage and to my neighbor's house, I realize that the postal service driver has just delivered the mail. I put the tool down, grab the mail, and fan through it. A letter advertising a rug-cleaning special catches my attention, and I realize that if I don't make the call immediately, it will never get done. As I go back in the house to make the call, I notice the pile of laundry that hasn't been placed in the washer because there was no laundry detergent. I think, *If I get the detergent first, then the clothes can wash while I finish whatever else I am doing.* On my way to the supermarket, I see the car wash sign flashing and think, *What's five minutes to put the car through the car wash?*

Get the point? This story may be an over-exaggeration, but it's not too far off from the reality of how distractions can easily derail us. Many of us, in one way or another, can relate to similar situations. At the end of the day, the garage is *still* not cleaned, the tool is *still* not returned, the call *still* hasn't been made, the laundry detergent *still* hasn't been bought . . . yet I am tired and frustrated. Let me remind you that the greatest obstacle to finishing what you start is often your own fears, anxieties, doubts, and distractions. These struggles can paralyze progress.

So, now that you have experienced a taste of what the future holds but find yourself at the crossroads of decision-making, you can choose to succumb to distractions and back into a place of confinement and complacency, or you can march forward into God-given opportunities, into the realization of dreams and endless possibilities.

This does not mean that you cannot multitask. However, it does mean that, unlike my metaphor of dealing with ongoing distractions and no accomplishments to show for it, you must focus on making progress on those things you know are connected to your God-size dream. It may very well mean that you say no to some things. It may mean that you become fully aware of those things that can distract you, and keep your focus on the goal!

Abraham's challenge to remain obedient in sacrificing his son speaks to this conundrum. The biblical narrative reminds us that although Abraham took with him two servants on his journey to the sacrifice, he didn't allow them to trek the rest of the way with him up the mountain. I am wondering if his servants would have attempted to talk Abraham out of the sacrifice had they been present.

We must stay clear of the voices that attempt to talk us out of our obedience. Keep in mind that *you* are the one who received the God-size vision. *You* are the one who received the God-size dream. Therefore, those who are not privy to the magnitude of what is within you will not understand the magnitude of the sacrifices you need to make to remain focused till the end. This dimension is so crucial that what you do here will determine whether you experience the fullness and fulfillment of what you have been called for or delay the process.

Let me warn you. The dimension of obedience is by far the most difficult dimension to live through. It is a tiring dimension. It is a sacrificial dimension. It is often a lonely dimension. At least the second dimension—a quite difficult one—came on the heels of receiving the dream or vision. The fourth dimension, however, comes on the heels of taste. It comes on the heels of feeling like you were almost there, and then BOOM, just like that, the narrative has shifted.

A biblical narrative about a man with a God-size vision named Nehemiah speaks to this tiring crossroads. Nehemiah 4 relates the story of a people who set out to rebuild the walls of Jerusalem. In alignment with Nehemiah's God-size dream, they set out to rebuild a city that had been utterly destroyed and reestablish a place of security against their enemies. Their vulnerability had lasted long enough. It was time for a God-size vision to be fulfilled. "So we built the wall, and the entire wall was joined together up to half its height," they said because, "the people had a mind to work" (v. 6, NKJV). Notice what happened after that: "Then Judah said, 'The strength of the laborers is failing'" (v.10, NKJV).

A combination of trash, mockery, threats, and exhaustion (vv.10-12) became a perfect storm against their progress. What will they do? Will they stop? Will they give in to fear and trepidation? Or will they recalibrate and re-strategize as they heed the encouragement of the one who had been given the dream? They did the latter. They recalibrated, re-strategized, and set out to finish what they had started.

The dream was too great. The future of their families depended on it. Despite the challenges, they needed to quiet the opposing voices and step out in obedience to finish what they had started.

Following through requires a resilient mindset. So, stay focused, avoid distractions, and don't give up easily. Fulfillment and fullness are on their way!

What opposition are you up against? What voices must you silence to remain focused on your God-size dream? What distractions have attempted to creep in and derail you from experiencing the fullness of your God-size vision?

///

The God-size dream—the God-size vision—is too grand to be aborted because of failure.

///////

For us, we have the benefit of already knowing the rest of our protagonists' stories. Not so for them. They had to push through and believe by faith alone that the dream would become a reality, that the vision would be fulfilled. For many of us, knowing the outcome encourages us to press forward. But what happens when you must move forward in obedience when all you have is the initial dream? What happens when all you have is a reminder of the vision? You must muster up the courage and focus to remain steadfast; you must remember you are just in another dimension in the process of fulfillment.

FAILURE IS NOT THE END

Thus far, we have focused on Joseph's resilience to remain faithful to his character and integrity. I have pointed out the people of

Judah's obedience to the voice of Nehemiah to finish what they had started. I have also reviewed Abraham's obedience demonstrated in his willingness to sacrifice Isaac. All those scenarios are filled with steadfastness, resilience, and tenacity. But what if your track record is replete with less-than-perfect decisions? What if, unlike Joseph, you have stumbled, faltered, and failed? My message to you remains the same. Finish what you have started. The God-size dream—the God-size vision—is too grand to be aborted because of failure. God's faithfulness exceeds our fears; it exceeds our disobedience. As long as we have the wherewithal to get back on track and continue to believe that the God-size dream is still alive despite our setbacks, God will take over and bring the dream to its fullness.

Your past mistakes will not derail your future fulfillment!

Let us not forget that Abraham stepped out in obedience to sacrifice his son Isaac but only after he recovered from a costly mistake. He heeded the voice of his doubting wife, Sarah, who thought she could not possibly conceive a child in her old age. In doing so, he succumbed to sleeping with her servant Hagar, who gave birth to a son they named Ishmael. Although the entire narrative may not align with our contemporary social and cultural narrative, at the time, it played out in ways that bore consequences with long-term ramifications.

Did Abraham and Sarah's poor choices negate the fulfillment of their God-size vision? No! Despite their setback, they understood that failure was not the end. If they were going to witness the realization of their God-size vision, then they would need to keep believing that past mistakes could not derail their future fulfillment! This applies to you as well! Your past mistakes will not derail your future fulfillment!

As we move forward through the dimension of obedience, let us glean from the victories of those who preceded us. The magnitude of realized God-size visions and dreams helps us understand that when you persevere, you create a ripple effect. Your resilience, tenacity, and accomplishments serve to inspire others and set new standards. So, when faced with opposition, remember that finishing what you have started is more than a personal achievement—it is a gift to the world. Trust your readiness, embrace setbacks, and keep moving forward.

17

NUMBER TWO PERSON IN A NUMBER ONE WORLD

*"Remember, even the number two pencil is
essential for writing awesome stories!"*
—Author Unknown

The fourth dimension of obedience is inevitable in our journey toward fulfillment. It serves to test our resilience, our tenacity, and most of all, our faith. It not only tests our resolve in various areas, but it is also a training camp. This dimension tests how you handle challenges, someone else's business and the adherence to the God-size dream itself. It is the epitome of this scripture: "You have been faithful over a little; I will set you over much" (Matthew 25:21, ESV).

As you consider how to navigate this most difficult dimension of obedience, let me challenge you to make up your mind to become the best number two person in a number one world. What does that mean? It means that in a culture where people often seek to shine, to be first, to be noticed, and to be the number one person, choose instead to be the number two person. In a world that often celebrates the spotlight, the number two person—the trusted lieutenant, the right-hand man—might seem less glamorous. However, being the best number two is not only essential but also profoundly impactful.

Seek to be the one who serves instead of being served. Seek to be the one who points to the successes of someone else. Seek to handle someone else's business with excellence. The obedience you display throughout this dimension can very well open the door to the next.

I can share countless stories about how people infused with God-size dreams—with God-size visions—excelled at being a number two person. In doing so, the fourth dimension became not only their training camp but the very platform that launched them to the fulfillment of their dreams and visions.

Let's analyze our protagonist, Joseph, for instance. Not once throughout his entire life journey do we see him excel as the number one person. Yet, the responsibilities and authority he possessed created such an impact that it prevented what could have been a destructive future for an entire generation.

Within the dimension of taste, we read about Joseph's ability to protect his character and integrity by fleeing Potiphar's house. Although he fled without much preparation or advance notice, he did not go empty-handed. Maybe in a physical sense, yes. (He did not leave with physical possessions . . . or at least not that we know of.) Yet, he left with a wealth of management experience that would become part of his resume for the fulfillment of his dreams.

Did we forget that Joseph arrived at Potiphar's house as a slave? Yet, his excellent spirit made room for Potiphar to trust him with his entire household. Let's not move too quickly past this transition in Joseph's life. His condition did not determine his level of excellence. It was his character that determined it. He could have been bitter. Instead, his environment made him better. Imagine if he would have complained, at the very least, or even greater, sabotaged what had been entrusted to him because of bitterness. Imagine if he would have allowed the environment to determine his level of service. He would have missed out on the training that would later serve to fuel his success.

How about you? How do you deal with adverse circumstances in your life? Do you kick and scream and become bitter? Or do you view them via a lens of endless possibilities? Do you view them as an opportunity for training and advancement? Joseph served with excellence, and it was reciprocated in ways that exceeded his expectations.

Joseph's ability to be the best number two person became his modus operandi. After fleeing Potiphar's house, he was sent to jail because of Potiphar's wife's accusations of rape against him. Once again, he could have become bitter. Instead, he became better—to the extent that he earned the respect and admiration of the prison warden.

The biblical narrative reminds us that "The LORD was with Joseph and made him successful in everything he did" (Genesis 39:23, NCV). Wait, did you catch that? The favor and success of the One who provides God-size dreams do not occur outside of the efforts of the one who has been given the dream. God's success was over everything Joseph *did*. In other words, Joseph was not idle. Joseph did not just sit around wallowing in the consequences of false accusations. No! Joseph *did*! When he did—when he acted— success followed.

Joseph's obedience to serve—to be the best number two person—became a catalyst for promotion. The warden trusted Joseph to the extent that he paid no attention to anything that was under Joseph's care!

Can you be trusted in adverse circumstances? Can you be trusted in a work environment that is less than ideal? What is your behavior in places that challenge you? Could it be that many of us may have missed opportunities for advancement because we react negatively to conditions rather than rise above them?

//

When circumstances are less than ideal, you still get up, dress up, show up, and refuse to give up.

//////////

Remember the part-time job I wrote about in chapter 13? That evening job was not ideal. Sitting at a call center selling credit cards after a full day's work was not my idea of success. Like many who worked there, I could have walked in like I had just rolled out of bed. I could have made just enough phone calls to get by night after night. But I refused to be like everyone else. I learned at a young age that, figuratively speaking, when life gives you lemons, you don't become bitter and throw them away—you take them and make refreshing lemonade. You give your best. I learned that when circumstances are less than ideal, you still get up, dress up, show up, and refuse to give up.

I could not have imagined that out of all the representatives in that call center, I would receive a call to meet with the senior vice president and be promoted to the top position at that location. I quickly realized that there is always someone watching. Quite often, and unbeknownst to us, people watch our actions, listen to our rhetoric, observe our demeanor, and seek to know how we handle adverse circumstances. All it takes is for the Dream-Giver to have the right person at the right time to serve as the catalyst that launches you toward the fulfillment of your God-given dream.

The promotion I received at that firm was not the fulfillment of a God-given dream. But it undoubtedly served as a training camp that would lead me to another position, that led to another, and another, and another. Each time an advancement came, I walked away, knowing that I had given my best. I walked away with more knowledge, more wisdom, and a greater sense of what loomed on the horizon.

As we delve deeper into Joseph's lifestyle, we discover that, time and time again, conditions weren't ideal. Everything Joseph excelled at happened in the middle of a challenge. Can you imagine landing in a prison, being given charge over prisoners, and then proceeding to serve them while no one is serving you? This is indeed the model of being the best number two person in a number one world.

Let me explain. Joseph– the man who has been given a God-size dream—has now been entrusted with overseeing other prisoners.

Two of the prisoners who were in the prison had experienced a confrontation with the king that landed them in jail. Coincidentally, each of the two prisoners had dreams while in jail. When Joseph saw that they seemed worried, he inquired about their condition. They proceeded to share their dreams with Joseph, and Joseph interpreted them.

Joseph's actions do not cease to amaze me. It takes someone committed to being the best number two person to act and serve the way Joseph did. How can a man with a God-size dream interpret someone else's dream while no one is interpreting his? Could it be a test of how we handle other people's dreams while our dreams go unfulfilled?

Once again, Joseph could have been bitter. He could have thought, *Why should I care about their dreams? I, too, had dreams, and here I am in prison!* He could have thought, *Why should I serve anyone? The last time I did that, someone lied about me, and it landed me in prison!* But here is where I remind you that your God-size dream is too big to allow bitterness, anger, remorse, or complacency to keep you from giving your very best in adverse situations. You never know how the Dream-Giver will connect the dots and use your obedience to become the best in your worst moments and launch you to fulfillment.

HIDDEN DOORS

I believe there are hidden doors behind acts of obedience, pathways that are only accessed once steps of obedience are taken. A few years ago, just like how Joseph fueled someone else's dream, I was prompted to invest in a colleague's dream. I had served with him in multiple capacities over the years. He was the president of a national organization and was hosting a board meeting combined with a conference in a state on the other side of the nation. I saw an ad for his conference come across my social media platform. The moment I saw the post, I felt a prompting to attend. I had not been invited. I was not a guest speaker. Nor was I part of the board of directors at that time. Yet, I felt something tell me, *Sometimes, it is good to invest in other people's dreams, not just your own.*

Attending the conference would require an investment on my part. It meant that I would have to book a round-trip flight, book a hotel, pay a registration fee, and, of course, cover any additional personal expenses. I shared my prompting with my wife, and although she found it a bit odd, she said, "If that is what you feel, then you should go!" Thank God for wives who trust their husband's promptings.

The time came, and I flew out to the event. Other than experiencing a couple of great conference sessions, an evening concert, reconnecting with several people I knew, and some general networking, I didn't experience anything out of the ordinary. As a matter of fact, the evening before the day I had to fly out, I ran into the president of the organization, who asked me, "What are you doing here?"

Initially, I thought, *How rude!* But after a brief conversation, I understood that he was simply shocked to see me.

He said, "You should have told me you were coming! We could have connected earlier. . . ." I welcomed the pleasantries but thought nothing more of them.

A few days after returning home, I received a call from the president of the organization. He said, "I am going to share something extremely important with you. I need you to give it thought and call me back before the end of the day!" Before I could ask what was so urgent, his next sentence changed my life. He said, "I have been presented with an incredible proposition, and it requires that I offer an opportunity to several people. As I thought about whom to consider, I pictured you at my recent conference and immediately knew that you had to be one of them!"

His next few words changed the trajectory of our ministry at the time. He offered an opportunity to air a one-hour weekly program on a national television station. Wait, there is more! We would record our program at their studios in New York City with some of the best equipment and staff in the industry, all for the grand price of zero dollars. Each episode was probably equivalent to ten thousand dollars. I was speechless!

Having our own television program had been a dream—a dream that had gone unnoticed and unanswered until I invested in someone else's dream. Little did I know that my obedience to that prompting—that still small voice within—would serve as the fertile ground where my dream would be birthed. One act of obedience multiplied into thousands of dollars of free television programming and a global impact on the lives of thousands upon thousands of people.

What if I had disobeyed that prompting? What if I had concerned myself with the cost of investing in someone else's dream? What if I had chosen to ignore the prompting and stay at home just because I had no role to play in the conference? I cannot express how glad I was that at that moment, everything I had done had nothing to do with me. It had nothing to do with investing in some personal dream. Had it been my conference or some other event, I would have been the number one person. That was not the case. I was simply a number two person, serving someone else's dream.

///

Your dreams are not just personal dreams intended for personal gratification. They are grand and intended to impact others.

/////////

Joseph was no different. (Please pardon the spoiler alert!) I wonder if Joseph ever imagined that the unselfish act of interpreting the dreams of two individuals who were in the same boat as he was—serving as prisoners—would become the open door to free him and launch him into the fulfillment of his God-size dreams.

Please do not miss the details delineated throughout this dimension. God-size dreams—God-size visions—are so powerful that they require intentionality. You cannot ignore promptings when you navigate the dimensional journey toward the fulfillment of dreams. You cannot live as a proverbial cookie-cutter individual. You cannot live like everyone else and expect God-size results. You are different! Your dreams are not just personal dreams intended for personal gratification. They are grand and intended to impact others. They are intended to make a difference for generations to come.

THE DELIVERY BOY

Countless resilient people throughout history have learned the art of obedience. Their obedience has launched them into living out God-size dreams. One such person is found in a biblical narrative

about a young boy who served his father in the shadows—in anonymity—while his brothers basked in the spotlight. The young
man's name is David, and his story is found in the Bible within the
first book of Samuel.

I will not outline his entire narrative. Let me pick up after a seer
(a prophet) singled him out and prayed for him, and, in an act of
divine calling, poured oil over his head. At that moment, David
was given a God-size dream. He had been separated for something
greater. Yet, the story reveals that despite his spotlight moment in
front of his family, he went back to serving his father by taking care
of his sheep. David went back to being a number two person in a
number one world.

One day, his father asked him to take lunch to his brothers who
were on the battlefield fighting a consistently antagonizing enemy.
In obedience to his father, David, lunch basket in hand, trekked out
to the battlefield to serve his brothers' lunch.

As he approached the margins of the battlefield, he heard
Goliath, a gigantesque man on the enemy's side, taunting and
mocking the God whom David served—the God of Abraham, Isaac,
and Jacob, the God of the Israelites. The time came when David had
heard enough. He could not believe how his brothers and every
other soldier could stand by as Goliath mocked them day and night.
Without hesitation, he set out to go against the giant.

What prepared him for such an internal prompting? Was it his
military preparation? No! He did not have any. Was it his size and
stature? No! He was infinitesimal compared to the giant! What
was it? David articulates it all too well—it was the preparation he
received while serving his father and taking care of his sheep. In a
place where his accomplishments went undetected and outside of

the spotlight, he was fending off lions and bears to keep his father's sheep safe. Little did he know that that less-than-ideal environment would become the training camp that would set him on his course to the fulfillment of a God-size dream.

Again, spoiler alert! David defeated the giant. In doing so—in obeying his father and serving his brothers' lunch—he found himself in a once-in-a-lifetime opportunity that would set him on track to see the fulfillment of the very thing he had been set apart to do.

> **If serving was not beneath David, who became a mighty and extremely successful king, then it should not be beneath you or me.**

What if David's reaction to his father would have been, "Why do I have to take the lunch?" or "I have sheep to take care of. Send someone else." What if the ceremony that set him apart would have instilled pride in him and provoked him to think, *I am no longer a number two person; I am number one!* He would have missed the opportunity that emerged from serving someone else. He would have missed the prompting to go against a giant that others were afraid to confront.

If serving was not beneath David, who became a mighty and extremely successful king, then it should not be beneath you or me. If his ceremonial calling to the title of "king" did not quench his desire to be obedient, then neither should our positions, titles, and accomplishments keep us from obedience. One act of obedience could be the catapult into the fulfillment of your God-size dream.

18

SACRIFICE

"Nothing great was ever accomplished without making sacrifices."
—Author Unknown

"He who would accomplish little need sacrifice little;
he who would achieve much will sacrifice much; he
who must attain highly must sacrifice greatly."
—James Allen

Acts of obedience can include acts of sacrifice. What if a sacrificial act was the threshold between the dimension of obedience and your next dimension, and the difference between remaining where you are or moving forward? At first glance, sacrifices may seem daunting. However, they are not inherently negative. To make a sacrifice is to make a conscious choice to prioritize certain goals over others. So, if you are going to see the fulfillment of God-size dreams —God-size visions—expect to make sacrifices.

The biblical account of one of our protagonists—Abraham—is a perfect example of the intersection between obedience and sacrifice. As you navigate the journey toward the fulfillment of a God-size vision, Abraham's willingness to sacrifice his son Isaac, known as the *akedah* or the binding of Isaac,[4] offers profound insights into the importance of sacrifice. Abraham was willing to hold captive—to bind—the very thing he loved and put it on an altar to obey what he sensed was God's direction for his life.

Throughout the last few chapters, I have presented the distinction between Isaac as a taste of a greater promise and Isaac as the fulfillment of a promise. We know, from the biblical text, that the promise to Abraham *was not* that he would simply have a son, but that he would become a great nation (Genesis 12:2). So why would a loving God demand such an extreme sacrifice by asking Abraham for his son? We already know how the story ends. We are privy to the fact that Abraham did not have to follow through on the sacrifice.

Sacrifice is an expression of commitment and loyalty.

So again, why the demand? The answer lies in faith. God was not trying to be cruel. Instead, the Giver of the God-size vision knew all too well the magnitude of what Abraham was called to accomplish. So, had Abraham staunchly held on to Isaac out of fear, how

---

4 "Akedah," *Encyclopaedia Britannica*, last updated 28 Jun 2024, https://www.britannica.com/topic/Akedah.

could he be trusted to handle greater things? Unlike Abraham, it isn't often the size of our vision that stagnates our progress but our inability to live life with an open hand. We often receive gifts, blessings, or opportunities that never belonged to us in the first place. We then proceed to staunchly hold on to them for fear of losing what we have. We hold on to them as if the same God that made a way for the initial opportunities is not the same God that can make a way for greater things. Abraham's unwavering obedience demonstrated that true greatness often requires stepping into the unknown, guided by faith, with the initial God-size vision embedded deep within our soul as our guide.

Abraham's willingness to sacrifice his beloved son underscores the concept of sacrifice as devotion. Sacrifice isn't merely about giving up something valuable. It is an expression of commitment and loyalty. Sometimes sacrifice is about setting a standard that has not been set before simply because of a commitment to see the fulfillment of something much greater than yourself. Like Abraham, you may be prompted to make sacrifices that you do not yet have a pattern or point of reference for. Yet, you know that you must make them if you want to see the fulfillment of your God-size vision.

I am reminded of another VIP in the Bible named Joshua. He had been accustomed to being the best number two person in a number one world. He was number two to a man named Moses. Yet, when Moses died, he was left with the task of leading thousands of people into a land God had promised them. Here's the thing. He had never been down that road before. So, officers under his leadership gave the people very specific instructions to follow so that they could accomplish what had been promised (Joshua 3).

Similarly, on our journey to fulfillment, there are things we encounter that we don't have a model behavior for. So, considering that God-size dreams require God-size intervention, we must be open to the prompting that leads us down unfamiliar paths.

Like Abraham, you, too, may initially question the purpose of making sacrifices. In hindsight, you realize that your actions modeled behavior for others to follow. You realize that your actions set the standard for others to emulate; that a simple vision may require minimum action, but a God-size vision often requires extreme sacrifices. I know the sting of such sacrifices all too well.

BECOMING

There wouldn't be enough space in the manuscript to count the ways I've had to make sacrifices on this road to see the fulfillment of a God-size vision, especially as an intrinsically introverted, bullied little boy from a one-square-mile city in New Jersey who could have been a statistic of status quo living.

Early on in life, I learned a valuable lesson. I learned that if you cannot find the help you need to navigate the journey to maturity, then you make whatever sacrifices necessary and become that person. Sometimes, your success will come from *becoming* the model rather than *waiting* for someone to model behavior. You must become it. Through divine direction, you become what you need. You become the model for someone else. You set the path for others.

I had to live out that principle of *becoming* several times in my life. One such moment came early on during my vocation as a pastor. Imagine a pastor in his twenties desperately needing and seeking a model of leadership so that I could thrive. I am not talking about people you read about or watch YouTube videos about. I am talking about the kind of people you can call and whose wisdom you can glean from when you need it most—people with no ulterior motives.

At the time, I did not have the budget to pay some of the honorariums and travel expenses associated with bringing high-caliber leaders to conferences or special events. I knew how important it was to have voices, other than my wife's and mine, speaking and sharing wisdom with our leadership and congregants in general. But for whatever reason, I felt stuck. I felt as though I couldn't connect with the right people, or the timing was off. Either way, I felt alone on a difficult journey with only God to pull on.

In hindsight, I now understand I was meant to go through that season and experience what I now call the dimension of obedience. Maybe it wasn't that people were unavailable. Maybe I was just blind to the options available to me so that I could obtain a greater understanding of what it meant to make sacrifices. Whatever the case, I went for a long walk one day and cried out to God, "Where are the people who can come to my rescue when I need them most?!" I exclaimed. "Is there anyone out there who is prompted to pick up the telephone and say, 'I felt nudged to call you and offer any help that I can'?" I continued to rattle on.

As my tirade ensued, I questioned people's motives. "It's a shame I cannot bring the quality of people I would like to bring to speak because I cannot afford them," I ranted. At that moment, I had to catch myself. I could not allow my unmet needs to become bitterness. I could not begin to look at things through a negative lens and accuse people without any justifiable cause.

As I vacillated between a cry for help and a pity party, I thought of Joseph. Yes, our biblical protagonist Joseph. I wondered if that was how he felt while in prison interpreting other people's dreams while no one was there to interpret his. I wondered if that was how he felt when those whose dreams he interpreted were released from prison (one of them did lose his life), while *he* remained forgotten.

I sensed God respond immediately with a rather peculiar yet precise prompting: *become that person!* Wait! What? I am crying out for help, and instead of receiving the help I need, I am instructed to become the very person I am looking for. Well, that was *not* the answer I was looking for! But somehow, in a very odd kind of way, I was relieved. I somehow knew that this dimension was bigger than me. It was bigger than my temporary problems. There was a lesson in the making, and I was about to find out what it was.

The next morning, as I was sitting in silence during my usual time of devotional, prayer, and meditation, I was quickened by the thought of a pastor in another state. I had not been thinking of him, nor had his name come up in any recent conversations. So, I knew at that moment that I should call him.

I immediately picked up the phone and called him. To my surprise, he picked up. I'm not sure why I was expecting to get his voicemail. After some very brief and cordial salutations, I was honest with him. I said, "I am not exactly sure why I am calling. I was sitting here doing my daily devotional, praying, and meditating, and felt prompted to call you! So, maybe this means nothing," I continued. "If that is so, just know that there is someone out there who just thought of you and is praying for you!"

There was a long pause. I thought maybe we had gotten disconnected. But just as I was getting ready to probe if he was still on the line, he said with a sobbing tone, "I can't believe this call!"

"What do you mean?" I asked, wondering what was happening.

He said, "I was just crying out to God asking, 'Is there anyone out there who hears from You and would be obedient enough to pick up the telephone and offer help or a word of encouragement?'"

I was speechless.

I was humbled by such a divine moment! Everything I was going through was dwarfed in comparison to the mixture of humility *and* privilege I sensed at that moment. Without hesitation, I offered to provide the very thing I had been asking for. I made it clear that I was not looking for a speaking engagement or anything of the sort. I simply said, "If I can be of service to you, your leadership, or your congregation, please know that I am here. You do not have to worry about an honorarium or covering any costs. This is totally on me. I am here to invest in your vision!"

As if this had been an answered prayer, he took me up on my offer. I was not in a position to freely make such sacrifices. I was young! I was just getting started, and I needed help. Yet I knew that's exactly what this was—a sacrifice.

As this same scenario played out multiple times with different people around the nation, I quickly realized that the purpose behind all of this was not to simply travel the nation or the world with no concern for honorariums or travel expenses. I knew it was a test of obedience. It was a test of becoming. Could I become the very person I was seeking? Could I model the behavior I was desperately needing?

Every single time I have been prompted to take a big step of faith, the outcome has been supernatural. The relationships I have developed and the people I have divinely met while stepping out in obedience have been invaluable.

Interestingly, the more I *became* the person with the qualities I was seeking, the more God providentially made a way to meet my needs. Here is one example of the many times I have witnessed such a phenomenon.

It was a Wednesday night during those early years when I would go on my prayer walks (sometimes they were more rants and tirades than they were prayers). A woman who did not attend our church walked into a mid-week service we were having and asked to see my wife and me after the service. As if desperate to get a hold of one of us, she approached us in the sanctuary just as the service had come to an end.

She said, "I am here because while praying yesterday, I was prompted to write out this check and bring it to you! I am not sure why the odd amount, but I am just being obedient," she added without any hesitation.

///

What we make happen for others, God can make happen for us.

///////////

When we opened the check, it was for the exact balance for the carpeting ordered two days prior for the new worship sanctuary we had been building for the last six months. We thought we would have to raise those funds. As a newer church with young pastors, we had been planning and strategizing, but truthfully, we were also moving in faith. Not blind, ignorant faith. Not the kind that makes ignorant moves but the kind that requires much stretching beyond our comfort zone.

As my wife and I looked at the check, speechless, I was reminded that obedience has a way of reciprocating. What we make happen for others, God can make happen for us. What we, in obedience, become for others, God will cause others to become for us.

Could it be that the next dimension awaits on the other side of the sacrifices we are willing to make? Not because we are asked to make sacrifices as a form of cruel and unusual punishment. No! But because if we are going to be entrusted with greatness, then we cannot allow the things we should willingly let go of to own us. Weren't those God's words to Abraham right as he was about to sacrifice Isaac:

> "Do not lay a hand on the boy! . . . Do not hurt him in any way, for now I know that you truly fear God. You have not withheld from me even your son, your only son. Then Abraham looked up and saw a ram caught by its horns in a thicket. So, he took the ram and sacrificed it as a burnt offering in place of his son." —Genesis 22:12-13 (NLT)

I can't help but wonder how long that ram was caught in the thicket. Had it been there in plain sight? Had he been blinded from it because he was so focused on being obedient to what he innately felt he had to do? Whatever the case or the reason, the ram waited on the other side of his obedience. Like Abraham, I have witnessed the proverbial ram many times. And just like Abraham, they have only come into plain view *after* acts of obedience. How about you? Could it be that your dimension of fulfillment awaits on the other side of *your* obedience?

19

YOUR DARKEST MOMENT

"Even in your darkest moment, remember, there is still a dream!"
—C. Olmeda

"Obscurity cannot hide a clear vision!"
—C. Olmeda

In life's darkest moments, when the weight of adversity threatens to crush your spirit, it's easy to lose sight of your dreams. Yet, it is precisely during these challenging times that your God-size dreams can shine most brilliantly. Remember, they are God-size dreams. They are greater than your limited capacity. God-size dreams require God-size strength. God-size dreams require God-size tenacity. That means that in those moments of despair when loss and hardship loom large, a profound tenacity arises that carries you through the storms of adversity. You may not come *out* of the storm, but you will make it *through* the storm!

Life's darkest moments come in a myriad of forms. They may manifest as personal tragedies such as the loss of loved ones, a debilitating illness, profound disappointments, or what may seem like shattered dreams. They may also emerge from external forces such as societal upheavals, economic crises, or natural disasters. In each instance, the darkness threatens to overwhelm and shroud aspirations in doubt and despair. Yet, within the depths of these experiences lies a transformative power. It is in these moments of desperation that your human spirit is tested and, paradoxically, strengthened. The resolve to endure and overcome is often born in the crucibles of these adversities.

What makes this dimension the darkest within the fifth-dimension model? It often lingers on the fringes of the fifth dimension. In this dimension, you are on the cusp of seeing the fulfillment of your God-size dreams. I have often wondered how many people have given up, taken their own life, aborted a dream, or acquiesced to the status quo, not realizing that the dark moments would not last forever.

I wonder if that is how Joseph felt. He had excitedly shared his dreams with his brothers while brandishing a multicolored overcoat that his father had given to him. That display of grandeur did not go over too well. He was thrown into a dry well and left for dead while his brothers sat and enjoyed a meal nearby (Genesis 37).

Who would display such heartless behavior? That level of hard-heartedness displays the level of disconnect that overtakes someone's emotions when jealousy and contempt are present. Sadly, Joseph had to endure such atrocities as an innocent man. How does one process such a turn of events? One thing is to endure consequences because of personal improprieties. Another thing is to find yourself suffering because of someone else's selfish, jealous, and destructive behavior.

Thankfully, out of a random act of mercy, his brothers chose to sell him as a slave instead of leaving him for dead. By now, you know how that story ended. Despite Joseph's model behavior, his master's wife wrongfully accused him, and he ended up in prison. One would think that such a dramatic and traumatizing turn of events would cause Joseph to become bitter. Why wouldn't he? He has endured betrayal, mistreatment, and lies and now must endure a jail sentence for something he knows he is innocent of.

Have you ever felt that way? Just when you have caught a break, that relief becomes short-lived after a turn of events? That is precisely what the fifth-dimension model depicts. If you are not careful, you can misconstrue this dimension of obedience, where challenges, pain, and obscurity seem to prevail, as the end of the proverbial rope. But what if I told you that in the master plan of God-size dreams, all things work together for good (Romans 8:28). Because the dimension of obedience is part of the process of seeing the fulfillment of your God-size dreams, attitude and behavior during this dimension matter.

I am not ignorant of the plethora of emotions that come with challenging times. Questions, pain, frustration, and even anger can emerge when those moments of pain and obscurity invade your life in unexpected ways. When they do, those emotions must be processed, communicated, and confronted. But they do not have to control you. If you can acknowledge that even those moments of obscurity can play a role in the fulfillment of your God-size dreams, then how you handle the process becomes of crucial importance.

The more I think of Joseph's process, the more I am convinced that the dimension of obedience is not exempt from the process of fulfillment. Instead, it is an integral part of the process. The dimension of obedience produces opportunities for resilience, growth, and a test of your character.

RESPONSIBILITY AND RESPONSE

To get a glimpse of how attitude categorically influences the fulfillment of a God-size dream, let's take a look at Joseph's process during one of his most difficult, cold, and obscure seasons in prison. Two key aspects of his journey stand out as worthy of observation—his responsibility and his response. How is it that someone who has endured such hardship remains so steadfast? His steadfastness is such that the divine Giver of his God-size dream grants him favor with the warden. Not just the type of favor that caused him to stand out from the other prisoners. No! This kind of favor granted him oversight of all that went on in the prison. The warden did not even have to pay attention to anything under Joseph's care!

> **You may not have any control over what someone does. But you have control over how you respond.**

That level of favor teaches us that Joseph's sense of responsibility remained intact even amid adversity. His attitude, his resilience, and his ability to handle everything that had been entrusted to him with excellence spoke volumes of his character despite his surrounding conditions. Little did he know that the very place that could have crushed his spirit and his dream would become the launching pad for his promotion.

Joseph's attitude teaches us that while it was someone's false accusations that landed him in prison, his character had everything to do with his response. You may not have any control over what someone does. But you have control over how you respond. You may not have any control over the unexpected personal tragedies or external forces that catapult you into moments and places of obscurity, but you can control your attitude in the process. It is at this juncture that faith will carry you through—faith in God, the Giver of your God-size dream. Your faith will provide a beacon of light in the bleakest of times. As you navigate the fourth dimension in faith, you will understand the purpose of suffering, that trials are not arbitrary but opportunities for growth and transcendence.

Faith imbues life's challenges with meaning and serves as a source of strength and comfort. In the depths of despair, it promises hope and renewal. Faith becomes the bedrock upon which God-size dreams are built. Remember, these are God-size dreams. They carry a multigenerational impact. They defy logic and circumstance and are fueled by a conviction that transcends the temporal. So hold on, because the fourth dimension does not last forever.

Nowhere within Joseph's narrative do we read that he was able to expedite the journey through such a daunting dimension. Nowhere do we read about an encouraging voice while he navigated such a cold and obscure time. Nowhere do we read that he had another dream reminding him that the future looked brighter. Nowhere do we read of a divine voice comforting him that everything would be okay. Nowhere do we read of a visit reminding him that he was not alone. No! Nowhere! Instead, he found himself in a world of silence—maybe not from the prisoners around him but from anything that reminded him that his life was not over.

That silence is indeed what makes this dimension such a difficult one. So, what will you do when the silence is so deafening that you feel as if you have been abandoned? You hold on to the initial dream! If you are yet to experience the fulfillment of your God-size dream and all you sense is silence around you, then you are traversing the fourth dimension of obedience. It means that if you can show resilience even in your darkest moments, it is only a matter of time before you will bounce back from adversity. Whether you have noticed it or not, resilience is a hallmark of the human spirit. You have been created to withstand opposition. It is part of your blueprint.

Resilience is a testament to our innate capacity for transformation and renewal. Resilience allows individuals like you and me to not only weather life's storms but to emerge stronger, wiser, and more determined. How many stories have yet to be written about people who have risen from poverty to prosperity? How many stories have yet to be written about communities that have rebuilt in the aftermath of devastation? Resilience embodies the triumph of hope over despair. It is this resilience that nurtures and sustains God-size dreams, allowing them to flourish despite the odds.

It is at this crossroad between where you are and where you are going that I ask you to stop and ponder your God-size dream. It is not a mere fantasy. Your dream is imbued with purpose and meaning. Remember, God-size dreams transcend personal ambition. They are dreams that inspire and uplift—that transcend the limitations that circumstances and adversity impose. What distinguishes personal ambition from God-size dreams is the capacity to endure. God-size dreams are not easily deterred by setbacks or failures but rather thrive amidst uncertainty and challenge. They are fueled by passion, vision, and an unwavering belief in the possibility of the extraordinary.

As you begin to ponder the magnitude of your God-size dream, your attitude, behavior, tenacity, and resilience rise to new levels. Focusing on the fulfillment of your God-size dreams may not expedite the process through your darkest moments. It may not exempt you from the hurt, pain, anger, and the plethora of emotions that come with this dimension. But it will prevent your spirit from succumbing to desperation and acquiescence to a substandard level of living. Your environment may dictate one thing, but your mind, faith, and resilience will dictate another.

Let me remind you that this fourth dimension of obedience is by far the most difficult dimension to navigate. There is no way around it! Yet, while the darkest moments may cast long shadows, they cannot extinguish the light of God-size dreams. Faith, resilience, and an unwavering belief in the potential for transformation will enable you and me to transcend adversity and strive toward greatness. Whether personal or collective, these dreams inspire hope, ignite passion, and propel us toward a brighter future. Therefore, rest assured that within every challenge lies an opportunity for growth. Let us embrace the darkness, not with fear but with courage and conviction. For it is in overcoming adversity that God-size dreams are forged.

If all you see is darkness and despair, if all you sense is loneliness and a deafening silence, then hang on. The fourth dimension will not last forever. If all you have to remember is a taste but not the fullness of your God-size dream, then hang on. The fifth dimension is on its way!

20

ONE MORE ACT OF OBEDIENCE

*"You may be one step of obedience away from
experiencing the fulfillment of your dreams!"*
—C. Olmeda

We are not quite there yet! I know, it would have been a relief to move from the dimension of obedience and into the dimension of fulfillment without waiting a moment longer. Yet, here we are, still lingering on the dimension of obedience. Why? Because this is what it feels like in real-time. We often desire those challenging moments of pain and obscurity to come to an end sooner rather than later because our time traversing through them seems like an eternity.

I cannot move through our protagonist Abraham's narrative so quickly that I lose the intensity of his ongoing challenges. I would imagine that he, too, felt weary as he trekked his way through the land of Moriah to a mountain he would be instructed to ascend.

Oftentimes, we get a sneak peek at someone's challenge and tend to minimize it. I have been guilty of thinking that maybe I would handle the situation differently if I were the one going through it. What I failed to realize is that people have a history of challenges we are not privy to. It compounds and sets the stage for their present challenges. So, we must be careful not to judge people based on incomplete narratives.

We can miss moments when people are at a breaking point. Compassion should lead the way with people because it is easy to misconstrue demeanor or distance as bad behavior. They may very well be going through challenges they find difficult to process. It is in those times when people need encouragers in their corner to see them through, not people who condemn how they present in their fight to the finish line.

You, too, must protect your heart by wisely choosing the people you spend time with during your proverbial home stretch. It is imperative to surround yourself with the right voice. Surround yourself with voices of encouragement and wisdom. I am not talking about isolating yourself from people who can provide wise direction and counsel. We need those people in our lives when we are going through trying times. But there is a difference between those who tell us what we need to hear with love and respect and those who speak with judgment and condemnation.

I can't imagine that Abraham looked at the call to embark on a journey to sacrifice his son as an isolated instance. Thus far, he has had to navigate the journey of failure after producing a child through the "bondwoman" (Genesis 21:9, NKJV). As if that was not painful enough, he had to put her and the son he had through her—Ishmael—out of the house to preserve his relationship with his wife Sarah and his son Isaac. What a conundrum! And now, just as he has become acclimated to life with his son, he is now tested to step out in one more act of obedience. Does it ever end?

Isn't that like our lives as we navigate the dimension of obedience? The challenges we navigate are usually not considered isolated incidences. Instead, they often seem like longitudinal occurrences that follow a pattern in one way or another. And just when we think that we have overcome one challenge, we are faced with one more act of obedience. One instance (amongst many) stands out for me as I recall my own journey.

A PERSONAL TEST

I was navigating the ins and outs of pastoral ministry as a young man in his twenties and, with that, the need for a ministry building. The small congregation we had been leading had now outgrown a small chapel in a space we shared with another congregation. Just as my wife and I were beginning to enjoy the beauty of growth within the ministry, we were asked to move from the ministry location without much notice. The trustee who handled the affairs for the congregation we were space-sharing with suggested that we had outgrown the facility and was concerned it would cause too much wear on their property.

With very little time to secure another location, we planned, prayed, and prepared several strategies to move forward. The challenge with most of our strategies was that they required a great deal of funds, funds we did not have.

Within a week's time, I was slated to attend a conference at a very large church within a six-hour driving distance from my home. On the second day of the conference, something unusual happened as I sat amid the crowd as a general conference attendee. The lead minister took to the stage to raise funds for the ministry. To get the full picture of what happened, I must be brutally honest. About ten minutes into his fund-raising presentation, I had just about had enough. The thoughts rising in my mind were certainly not aligned with those of a pastor who knew what it was like to raise funds.

The display of generosity I witnessed was like something I had never witnessed before, but what I witnessed and what I thought were in direct opposition to one another. My skepticism was at an all-time high. People were giving thousands upon thousands of dollars.

One man, in particular, was handed the microphone to share that he had been at last year's annual conference and had been prompted to give five thousand dollars, even though he also needed funds to expand *his* ministry. When he returned home, to his surprise, the funds he needed were generated in ways he did not expect. As such, he was back to give ten thousand more dollars.

Instead of being happy for him, I was skeptical. I thought things like, *Been there, done that; I've seen this too many times before!* I had been in environments like this before and felt somewhat desensitized to these stories, or perhaps subconsciously, I was a bit jaded because I, too, was in a position of needing funding and hadn't yet seen it. What was wrong with me? Why was I thinking like this? A moment later, I saw a young lady from the choir give money she had saved for her college tuition, and I thought, *Are you kidding?* Just as I judged her actions, someone from the balcony came down and sent a message to the minister who stated that the balcony person had been moved to pay that young lady's tuition for the upcoming semester. The more skeptical I became, the more the whole thing snowballed into a giving frenzy like I had never seen. The more people gave, the more I felt like a rebellious heathen.

It was then that I felt a subtle prompting, *Give all you have!*

I'm not going to fall for this, was my immediate reaction. Oh, the struggle! How could I be feeling or thinking this way when I, too, had taught others to live a life of generosity? Yet, at that moment, I felt as if this was some religious attempt to manipulate and raise millions of dollars.

The more I fought it, the more the prompting within me intensified, *Give all you have!*

Well, I thought, *I have a decision to make!* So, I said to myself, *What is the worst that can happen?* I rationalized my next move. If I gave it all just because I was lost in the moment from all the buzz, then I would be out a little over $800 (which is what I had in my pocket between cash and a check that had been given to me) for no good reason. But if it was a divine prompting challenging me to step out in obedience because something greater loomed on the horizon, then I could potentially miss out on something greater if I refused to give. The problem was that my realistic, common-sense—yet judgmental—thought process directly opposed any measure of faith I probably should have had.

Nevertheless, I decided not to err on the side of caution. I can't quite remember the exact amount. As such, with much hesitation (just being honest), I signed the check over, took all the money I had in my pocket, got out of my seat, and went to deposit the money in the basket the usher was holding near the front of the church.

Do you remember what I suggested earlier about the fourth dimension? It is by far one of the most difficult dimensions to navigate. It is here where you normally don't have anything to go on other than your initial dream—your initial vision. It is not uncommon to go through this dimension and feel like you can't sense God. It is not uncommon to seek encouragement and feel as if there is no one available. After going through this dimension, let me suggest that these unusual, dark, dreary, and often painful emotions are part of the process.

That is exactly how I felt as I walked down that aisle ready to step out in what I had decided was an act of obedience. I was hoping to feel at least some goosebumps. Maybe the minister would stop me and share with me some divine revelation about how I was doing the right thing! Nothing! Nada! Complete silence! Just my thoughts and I navigating through a sea of emotions and ultimately an act of obedience! One thing I knew for certain—we were in need of a bigger ministry space and a building to call our own, and what I had in my pocket was not enough to purchase it.

> **I returned home $800 and something dollars poorer but one act of obedience richer.**

As I walked back to my seat, I struggled with a mix of emotions ranging between a sigh of relief because I had stepped out and obediently heeded a prompting and the uncertainty of whether I gave because I was simply lost in the moment. The more I struggled, the more I knew I had made the right decision. The last thing I wanted to deal with was regret. I did not want to leave that place without having made the right decision or feeling like I should have. I did not want to leave wondering what the future would have held had I been obedient.

Let me make something clear before I share the outcome of this act of obedience. I don't believe that my prompting had anything to do with the minister, the needs or lack of needs for that ministry, or whether I agreed with what happened at that moment from a financial point of view. Many have definitive views on this subject, and I am okay with that. As you can tell, I struggled with the entire process. This is what I do know: the entire process had to do with my heart, my ability to be sensitive to a prompting aligned with a God-size vision, and a test of my faith more than anything else.

You know the outcome for Abraham and Isaac. God never desired to rob Abraham of his son. Abraham's process was a test of his faith. Was he going to hoard a single son, or was he going to believe for the God-size vision that had been promised him?

I returned home $800 and something dollars poorer but one act of obedience richer. I say that with confidence because my ride home solidified what I could not find at the conference—peace. As I drove back home with one of my staff members, I began to weep. I was in the middle of the interstate, and a strong presence overwhelmed me. What I thought I should have felt at the confer-ence I was now sensing in the privacy of a vehicle. I knew I was sensing God in a special way. I knew at that moment that my step of obedience held great significance. If nothing more—if the future held nothing else—I felt great that I heeded the prompting and that money (or lack thereof) didn't deter me.

Here is what I do not find coincidental. Within two weeks of my return, I received a call from my wife that she and one of our leaders had located a building they thought would be great for our ministry. It was roughly thirty-seven thousand square feet, compared to the two thousand square foot chapel we had been renting. It was in a prime location and was being sold for roughly $800,000. The square footage and location were wonderful! The money was another issue!

In a turn of events that still amazes me today, despite the reservations that the real estate broker and his counsel expressed to the owner of the building, we were able to secure the property on a rental basis for one year with a promise to purchase the building within the year.

As the year progressed, the owner of the building, an elderly Jewish fellow, asked my wife and me to meet him at his house for tea. He was not a Christian and had no vested interest in anything we were doing other than his desire to sell his property. As we sat down across from each other, like a father looking at a son, he looked at me and said, "Young man, I was counseled by my broker to refrain from entering a year-long lease (with the option to buy) with you and your congregation. But I must tell you. . . ." His eyes and voice exuded a certain sternness that thickened the environment. At that point, I was not sure whether he had good or bad news for me.

Whether coincidental or not, at that moment, I made the connection between my act of obedience to that providential moment.

"Despite my broker's counsel," he continued, "I want to move forward with selling you the building!" My wife and I looked at each other with a sigh of relief. "I don't know you very well, but I do know this. You have tenacity! I believe in you," he shared with a tender, fatherly voice. "So, there is one more thing," he continued, "I will sell you the property at the listing price, but I want to give you back two hundred thousand dollars to make the necessary improvements for your vision!"

As I sat there flabbergasted and with my heart pounding, I immediately thought, *What is 800 and something dollars compared to 200,000!* Whether coincidental or not, at that moment, I made the connection between my act of obedience to that providential moment.

Like Abraham, who raised his eyes and saw a ram caught in a thicket after the angel stopped him from sacrificing his son, I felt like I was looking at my ram, the replacement to the initial sacrifice. Maybe the ram had been there all along, but Abraham's attention was not drawn to it until he took one more step of obedience. Perhaps the owner intended to do what he did all along. Yet, I did not see the blessing until I heeded the prompting for one more act of obedience.

Since that time, I have been tested to the tune of thousands of dollars at different points in my life. Every time the prompting comes, I revert to a knowing rather than a feeling. That is, I don't depend on a feeling or an emotion to ascertain or validate another act of obedience. Rather, I revert to the God-size vision within me and move in faith. Time and time again, the outcome never disappoints.

> **The God-size vision is always greater than the level of sacrifice we are prompted to make.**

What final act of obedience is God prompting you about? What things have you been tempted to hold on to—to hoard—out of fear over what you may lose? Maybe it isn't financial. For some, it is forgiveness. For others, it is time or a talent they can contribute. Our call to obedience usually encompasses one of three areas: our time, our talents, and our treasures.

As you navigate this dimension with all its uncertainties and questions, let me assure you once again. This dimension does not last forever! However, if you are waiting for a feeling, an emotion, or a voice to confirm a prompt to act in obedience, you may wait for a very long time. I have found that this dimension is not based on emotions but on knowing by faith that the God-size vision is always greater than the level of sacrifice we are prompted to make.

I cannot end this chapter without a disclaimer. These steps of obedience must be contextualized into a modern-day New Testament narrative. Thus far, my Abraham example is an Old Testament (Hebrew text) contextualization that cannot be replicated within its context of human sacrifice or anything to that extent. You will never be prompted to sacrifice anything that would be detrimental to your well-being or hurtful to anyone else. Although I was not in a position to freely give $800, doing so did not hurt anyone. As I stated, I have found that the sacrifices we are often called to make deal with time, talents, or treasures (our finances). So, as you move forward, longing to come out of the dimension of obedience, don't be alarmed if you are prompted to one more act of obedience.

So, when you reach that place in this dimension—when you are faced with the hardest part yet—know that that's a great indicator that you are simply in that final phase of the obedience dimension.

If so, do not fear; the next dimension is the dimension of fulfillment, and once you arrive, the dimension of obedience will seem insignificant compared to living in the fullness of your God-size vision.

5TH DIMENSION

FULLNESS OR FULFILLMENT

DREAMS
&
VISIONS

FAILURE
OR
BETRAYAL

TASTE

OBEDIENCE

FULLNESS
OR
FULFILLMENT

IT WAS WORTH
THE PROCESS

"Trust the process; the outcome will be worth it!"
—C. Olmeda

Hurry! Get Up! It's time to shave and change your clothes! I wonder what raced through our protagonist Joseph's mind as he heard similar words! I would have loved to have been there to see the look on his face. I imagine that instead of a look of relief, he may have had a look of confusion! I wonder if he said, "Wait! What? Where am I going? What did I do?" I imagine that considering his encounters with betrayal, he may have thought, *Not again! What did I do now?*

It had been two years since he had interpreted dreams for the king's chief butler and chief baker whose apparent offenses had gotten them thrown into prison despite their positions with the king. One thing Joseph knew for certain—you don't mess with the king! Just as Joseph had predicted through his interpretation of their dreams, the chief baker was hanged, and the chief cupbearer had been restored to his butlership. After two years, the butler became the ticket for Joseph to be summoned from prison by the king!

As I read Joseph's story and felt excitement for his impending release from prison, I was tempted to exclaim, "Finally, he has reached the fulfillment of his dream!" Yet, that was not the case, but it did get him one step closer. Further, he had not come this far by coincidence. No! It was the result of an investment he had made in the life of the chief butler while in prison. Unfortunately, the moment the butler caught his break and was released, he forgot about Joseph. Joseph sat in prison for another two years, wondering how the butler could have forgotten about him.

Isn't that like many of our journeys? Just when we think we are about to catch a break, it evades us, and the fulfillment of those God-size dreams seems to escape our grasp. Don't worry! Don't fret! The timing for the fulfillment of your God-size dreams is perfect. As I alluded to in chapter 9, God is connecting the dots, and slowly but surely, the full picture is becoming clear.

It is here where the full picture of each dimension coming together begins to make sense. Independent of each other, each dimension becomes either a time of celebration or a time of despair. But collectively, they become a picture depicting a life of purpose, with all its glory, successes, pitfalls, challenges, and pain. They all come together to reveal a greater purpose.

It had been a thirteen-year journey for Joseph between his initial dream that his family would one day bow down to him and his release from prison. The initial dream is what catapulted the process. His haste to reveal the dream launched him into the dimension of betrayal. By divine providence, what could have crushed him promoted him. Subsequently, just as he has acclimated to a taste of success, BOOM! A false accusation lands him in prison. Now, once again, he has begun the climb to the peak of life's proverbial roller-coaster ride—a view he once tasted in Pharaoh's house.

Every dimension has added value to his life! His success is about to be unveiled in a greater dimension, not because he succeeded at the age of thirty when the king summoned him. No! Instead, his success has become clear because he has paid the price for thirteen years.

Wouldn't it be unfortunate to go through life kicking and screaming through every challenging dimension and never learn the lessons those dimensions could have taught you? Or worse, wouldn't it be unfortunate to navigate through life's most difficult moments and miss out on growth, maturity, and the opportunities that were hidden within the difficult dimensions? Yet, because you saw them as unfair, you sat on the margins of life, waiting for something better to happen instead of living a better way.

Imagine if that had been Joseph's approach. "Don't bother me with your dreams," he could have sneered back at the butler and baker while in prison. "I, too, had a couple of dreams and look where they landed me!" Had that been his approach, he would have erased the metaphorical dots connecting the greater story and purpose of his life, thinking they were not part of the bigger picture. He would have sabotaged a future that was being fulfilled with every bit of effort he put forth—he just couldn't see it yet!

What am I telling you? I am telling you that each dimension does not work independently of the others. Our lives have been a progression of dimensions that slowly but surely prepare us for the fulfillment of God-size dreams.

After Joseph was summoned to Pharaoh's palace, it would take another seven years before Joseph would witness the fulfillment of his dreams. Yet, in the process, he experienced unprecedented success. This tells me that chasing a dream was not his priority. Even if he attempted to, he couldn't; he wasn't omniscient. He could not see and predict the future to connect all the dots to materialize his God-size dreams on his own. Instead, his modus operandi was simply to be the best version of himself every step of the way. His best asset was his ability to seize one opportunity at a time.

As he is released from prison, he witnesses the sum of all the actions he has taken. His behavior in the initial palace while a slave has now prepared him for his newfound opportunity. His selfless behavior in interpreting other people's dreams, while no one was there to interpret his, is now the ticket that gains him access to the king's palace.

Every dimension has been a school filled with principles. Every dimension has propelled him closer to the fulfillment of his God-size dreams. I unequivocally believe that herein lies the difference between self-aggrandizing dreams and God-size dreams.

People who chase personal dreams with no longitudinal or eternal value and very little impact for generations to come seek fulfillment for *themselves.* Let me be clear. There is nothing wrong with pursuing a personal dream. But, ultimately, you should ask yourself: *What is the ultimate goal? Why am I chasing this dream? Does it have eternal value? Whom does it impact?*

People with God-size dreams seek to become the best version of themselves. Even when they don't know what the future holds or when their plans do not turn out as they had anticipated, they move forward with unbridled tenacity and resilience, unrestrained by anger or resentment, and certainly without hurting people along the way. They understand that their God-size dream—their God-size vision—transcends personal ambition.

//

Preparation precedes promotion!

////////

Before we delve further into the fulfillment of a God-size dream and the fullness of a God-size vision, let us consider several principles that have surfaced throughout the dimensions leading to the fifth dimension. I am convinced that without these principles, the fifth dimension would be delayed, at best, or at worst, entirely evaded.

- **The Principle of Adaptability**—Life will never go as planned. Because our lives are composed of our actions and the social and cultural impact of our surroundings, circumstances will arise that extend beyond our control. The question is, can you adapt? You do not need to acquiesce to certain environments or conditions to adapt.

  Joseph was able to thrive by implementing the principle of adaptability. He maintained his uniqueness—his character and his integrity—while adapting to environments that were not necessarily aligned with his principles. He was a

God-fearing young man, adapting to environments that were contrary to his beliefs.

- **The Principle of Faithfulness**—It is easy to be faithful when things go well, but can you remain faithful amid opposition? Joseph's faithfulness and loyalty earned him rank amongst the great. Faithful people are trustworthy, reliable, and dependable. He could be relied upon for his skills and depended on to go beyond the call of duty and demonstrate concern for the greater good. Joseph was faithful to his God and faithful to people.

- **The Principle of Stewardship**—I heard someone make a comment once about a vehicle that had been lent to a friend. The person said to the borrower, "Are you going to drive it like a rental (car)?" By this, he meant carelessly; like a rental car that did not belong to him. That was not the case with Joseph. Joseph handled other people's business with excellence. He was entrusted with a palace because of the principle of stewardship. He was entrusted with a prison and its prisoners because of the principle of stewardship. Ultimately, he was entrusted with an entire kingdom because of the principle of stewardship. I am convinced that because he handled other people's property with care, he was granted a wealth of property to call his own.

- **The Principle of Connectivity**—I cannot tell you how many people I have counseled, mentored, and corrected who have sabotaged relationships out of anger, resentment, and vindictive behavior. Today, they have a difficult time looking at those they hurt directly in the eyes. Some people cannot go visit certain businesses, cannot apply for certain jobs, or cannot attend certain functions because of the damage they have caused. Imagine if you were about to land the greatest deal of your life or the job you had always dreamed of, and the last person they call as a character witness is someone who cannot say one positive thing about you because of how you treated them.

People who follow the principle of connectivity do not burn bridges because they never know when they will need it to cross over. Despite what Joseph endured, he did not sabotage relationships. He somehow understood that vindication did not belong to him. Be the better person. Honor relationships. Forgive offenses. "Love your enemies and pray for those who persecute you" (Matthew 5:44, NIV).

- **The Principle of Preparation**—Preparation precedes promotion! Do not wait until an opportunity presents itself to begin preparing; it may be too late. Whether intentional or not, Joseph prepared for thirteen years before being given the opportunity to manage the resources that would later sustain a country. He then prepared for another seven years during which he implemented all sorts of wisdom and strategies that would serve to provide the necessary resources for a country and his family (yes, even those who betrayed him) during the severe famine.

Trust me; I am not exempt from these principles. Today, I am walking through the doors of opportunity that I have been preparing twenty years for. If you miss something on your journey toward fulfillment, make certain it is because the opportunity did not present itself, not because you were unprepared.

FULFILLMENT

As we come to understand what fulfillment and fullness look like and their implications for the future, let me remind you that dreams aren't fulfilled by happenstance. Dreams demand! Perseverance sustains us during storms. When obstacles arise, we must remember why and how we embarked on this journey to God-size dreams in the first place. Fulfillment isn't about smooth sailing; it is about weathering storms and setbacks with unwavering commitment. Each setback becomes a lesson. Each failure becomes a stepping stone toward mastery. Each betrayal becomes a platform for forgiveness.

As you begin to get a glimpse of fulfillment, know that it is the achievement of something desired, promised, or predicted. Yet, you must also realize that fulfillment in itself is not the end—the end of a dream or the end of life. There is more (more on this in a later chapter).

The fulfillment of God-size dreams goes beyond personal success; it is about making a difference. Fulfillers of God-size dreams use their influence to contribute to the greater good. Whether it is managing resources, building schools, planting churches or faith-based organizations, advocating for social change, or mentoring others, they recognize that dreams fulfilled are bridges of impact. Fulfillment isn't the end; it's a chapter in an ever-evolving story.

22

GREATER THAN *YOUR* DREAM

"'God's fulfillment always exceeds our expectations!"
—C. Olmeda

As we come out of the fourth dimension and into the fifth dimension of fulfillment—of fullness—we must ask ourselves if what we are celebrating is a personal ambition or the fulfillment of a God-size dream.

Dreams are often seen as aspirations, goals, or visions of what one hopes to achieve or become. At a personal level, these dreams are typically shaped by individual desires, experiences, and perceived limitations. They reflect our understanding of ourselves and the world around us, grounded in our human perspective and capabilities.

Conversely, God-size dreams transcend these personal boundaries. They are inspired and shaped by a higher purpose. They are inspired by divine guidance, destiny, or calling. These dreams challenge our limited understanding and stretch our faith and courage beyond what we can comprehend or achieve on our own.

That is not to say that divine guidance does not often work in tandem with personal passion; it does. Quite often, a God-size dream may evolve out of something you are passionate about, like helping the less fortunate, teaching, social change, mentoring, or other interests that move you to greater levels of engagement.

EXCEEDING EXPECTATIONS

That was certainly the case with what I thought was a personal dream. I received a call from the mayor of our city asking if I would attend a meeting with a group of clergy and other non-profit organization leaders. I agreed to attend, although I wasn't clear about the agenda.

It turns out that the mayor had a dream to see some sort of youth outreach program with a faith-based component developed within the city. He thought that if anyone was going to fuel sustainable change within the city, it was going to be the church at large.

Shortly after he spoke, I sat quietly, thinking about how I could contribute to his vision. As I thought about what to do, I quickly remembered that I had developed a strategy to reach our city's youth via a mentoring program. However, that plan had been on hold for many years and placed on the back burner because of everything else we were busy doing.

Immediately, I felt an internal prompting that nudged me, and in that subtle, internal voice that most of us recognize, it said, *Give it away!*

I thought, *Give it away? We will get to that as soon as things slow down a bit*, I responded internally.

Yet the nudging continued, *Give it away!*

Not knowing how the rest of the attendees would respond to my suggestion, I waited until the next day to call the mayor and tell him what I felt. I mentioned the mentoring model we had designed and that I would be more than happy to share it with him. I then offered to help in whatever way I could or team up with other leaders to make certain that his vision became a reality.

Within twenty-four hours of sharing my vision with the mayor, he called and asked if I had a nonprofit organization unrelated to any religious organization—what is known as a 501(c)(3) not-for-profit organization. Coincidentally, we had just finalized the process of securing a not-for-profit community development organization to reach out to the community through various outreach programs.

> **When you get out of your way to make other people's dreams come true, God will put people in your path to make your dreams a reality.**

What he said next caught me by surprise. "Wonderful!" He said with excitement, "What if I give you back your model along with $55,000 to begin the program?" I was speechless. I was immediately reminded of Joseph and how his selfless ability to interpret someone else's dream came back full circle to provide the open door he needed out of prison and into the palace.

I proceeded to connect with several other leaders who had attended the mayor's meeting to move beyond my own sphere of influence. I knew several of them well, while others I only knew of or was meeting for the first time. To my surprise, only two out of eighteen or nineteen leaders agreed to come on board.

There is a principle here that I have seen at work time and time again. When you get out of your way to make other people's dreams come true, God will put people in your path to make your dreams a reality. Herein lies the distinction between personal dreams and God-size dreams.

This chapter, however, is not simply about the fulfillment of dreams. It is about how the fulfillment of God-size dreams will always exceed our expectations. Unquestionably, a check for fifty-five thousand dollars exceeded our expectations. Yet, that was only the beginning. What we would witness as an organization certainly exceeded our expectations.

What started as a mentoring model designed to reach our city's youth evolved into a mentoring organization with a basketball component with our methodology reflected in the byline: "No Workshop, No Jump Shot!" For students to play basketball, they would have to attend workshops covering a broad range of topics: conflict resolution, relationship building, leadership development, and career apprenticeship, among others. The program got off to a great start but not without several challenges. First came a series of negative circulations from local journalists. They felt that a city program running on a Friday night would not thrive without challenges, with concerns ranging from misdemeanors to safety issues to a list of other reasons. Depending on the area in the city, these were valid concerns. We were cognizant that this would potentially

pose transportation issues for students because the sports component did indeed engage students at multiple locations until mid-
night. Yet, we also knew that this would become an alternative to
late-night hangouts. Despite the negative publicity, we were able
to work through the challenges and witness a successful season.

The mayor was thrilled that the program had gotten off to a
great start. So much so that roughly six months after the program
launched, he invited me to a press conference he was having the
day after his call. Considering the late invite, I assumed that he was
looking for representation from local leaders to support his agenda
during the press conference. Shockingly, right before the cameras
started rolling and he was about to take the stand, he leaned over
and whispered, "Get ready, I am going to have you share a few
highlights about the mentoring program!"

Wow! *No pressure,* I thought!

Thank God I learned early on as a leader that you should always
be ready with three points and a story. I proceeded to share three
points pertinent to the program's framework and a success story.

**The fulfillment of God-size dreams
will always exceed our expectations
or, even better, fulfill something we
didn't even know we wanted fulfilled!**

To my surprise, sharing a few highlights about the program is
not why he had invited me to the press conference. Instead, he

wanted to share that the city had earmarked an additional $200,000 of funding for mentoring initiatives, and considering our success, we were a great candidate for the funds. Within a couple of months, we had two more years of funding.

Again, the fulfillment of God-size dreams will always exceed our expectations or, even better, fulfill something we didn't even know we wanted fulfilled! We proceeded to mentor city students year after year. The program expanded from one mentoring site to five mentoring sites, covering three cities and witnessing over two thousand students go through the program. My dream to mentor students via a local church entity was exceeded by leaps and bounds to encompass a city-wide outreach that would connect law enforcement, local school districts, colleges and universities, and local businesses to reach a rising generation of youth.

I believe it's appropriate to extend an incredible amount of appreciation to a colleague and friend, Rev. Michael Comick. Rev. Comick believed in the vision, stuck by my side, and twelve years later, out of the initial two who joined me, he remains the only founding partner who still believes that despite the success we've already seen, our greatest days are still before us.

As we continue to delve deeper into the dimension of fulfillment, remember that fulfilling God-size dreams is a journey that transcends mere ambition and taps into the realm of purpose and divine orchestration. It invites us to consider the vastness of our potential when aligned to a higher calling. When we accept the invitation that catapults us beyond our perceived limitations, we also accept the challenge to think beyond ourselves and our immediate circumstances. This new level of thinking often requires a leap of faith, a willingness to step into the unknown, and a trust in something greater than our own abilities.

Like Abraham, who had to come out of his comfort zone and envision something much greater than he had ever imagined, you, too, can position yourself to envision a dream that exceeds your perceived limitations. When you do, let me remind you that the fulfillment of a God-size dream will exceed your expectations—hence, the second dimension of failure and betrayal and the fourth dimension of obedience. They become training camps, a place of isolation, questions, and uncertainty. They are not interruptions. They are part of the process. Nonetheless, through it all, you will receive the necessary bandwidth to handle the fulfillment.

THE DIFFERENCE

Regardless of what dimension you find yourself in today, here are some key distinctions between personal dreams and God-size dreams that surpass your personal limitations:

- **Expansion of Vision**—Personal dreams tend to be focused on individual achievement or fulfillment. God-size dreams expand our vision to include others, positively impacting communities, nations, or even the world.
- **Transformational Growth**—Pursuing God-size dreams challenges us to grow spiritually, emotionally, and mentally. It pushes us to confront our fears and insecurities and develop qualities such as resilience, perseverance, and compassion.
- **Divine Alignment**—Unlike personal dreams that rely solely on our efforts, God-size dreams are often accompanied by divine alignment. These are circumstances and opportunities

that unfold in unexpected ways to bring about the fulfillment of the dream.

- **External Significance**—While personal dreams may provide temporary satisfaction of recognition, God-size dreams have the potential for eternal significance. They contribute to a greater narrative of purpose and meaning that extends beyond our lifetime.

FAITH AND TRUST

You cannot expect to experience the fulfillment of a dream in ways that exceed your expectations without faith. At the heart of pursuing God-size dreams is faith—faith in God, faith in oneself, and faith in the journey ahead. It requires trusting that there is a greater plan unfolding, even when the path seems uncertain or challenging.

Abraham is a prime example of someone who understood this process all too well. He was called to leave his homeland and go to a place he did not know, with the promise that he would become the father of many nations. Despite his old age and the apparent impossibility of the promise, he believed.

Remember Nehemiah in chapter 3 of this book? While enjoying all the benefits of a palace, he heard from a conversation with his countryman that the wall of the city had been broken down and its gates burned with fire. The condition of the city stirred something within him that exceeded his personal limitations. Yet, he believed! He had faith! He had faith in God! He had faith in himself! He had faith in the journey! As such, every proverbial door that needed to be opened was opened. Every person he needed to gain favor with granted him favor. The resources he needed, he received. Strategies? Done! Manpower? Done! The fulfillment of the God-size dream that stirred within him exceeded his expectations. As a result, the walls were repaired in a record fifty-two days.

The fulfillment of God-size dreams—of God-size visions—will always exceed our limited mindset because they invite us into the extraordinary. They challenge us to see beyond ourselves and our circumstances and trust in guidance that transcends our understanding.

While personal dreams are important and valid, God-size dreams compel us to think bigger, love deeper, and impact greater. They remind us that our potential is not defined by our limitations but by our willingness to trust and follow where we are called.

Remember the negative publicity several local journalists attempted to spread regarding the mentoring program? Well, they failed to understand that God-size dreams do not normally acquiesce to the norm. Their fulfillment tends to exceed expectations. I witnessed that first-hand.

Just one year before composing this manuscript, I received shocking yet exhilarating news pertinent to the mentoring program. In a meeting with about a dozen chiefs of police from our surrounding cities and municipalities, as well as some other community leaders, our city's chief of police shared some startling statistics that I had not heard before. During the specific hours and months that we ran the program, youth misdemeanors and overall youth-related problems had decreased significantly in the communities where we had established it—an accomplishment he attributed directly to the program.

It seems like the media was wrong after all. When you dare to dream God-size dreams, you must close your ears to naysayers and to those who will attempt to sabotage your progress. Nehemiah knew this all too well. Despite many attempts to distract him from his assignment, he closed his ears to his scoffers and remained focused on the dream.

So, are you ready? Are you ready to experience fulfillment? Are you ready to experience fullness? Maybe not! Maybe this is new to you, and you have just been ignited and stimulated to dream God-size dreams. If so, arise! Come out of your comfort zone and dream. Dare to dream God-size dreams. When those dimensions of difficulty appear, know that they, too, will pass. Remain focused because the fulfillment of God-size dreams will exceed your expectations.

23

WHOSE DREAM IS
IT, ANYWAY?

"God-size dreams are intended to impact generations!"
—C. Olmeda

The true power of God-size dreams lie not in their ability to individually uplift and inspire us but in their capacity to create ripple effects that reach far beyond our own aspirations. When our dreams are limited in scope, focused solely on our personal happiness, advancement, or recognition, they risk becoming insular and disconnected from a more impactful human experience.

Moreover, dreams that lack a transcendent impact often fail to resonate with others on a meaningful level. They may inspire envy or admiration but do very little to foster a genuine connection. Conversely, God-size dreams that aim to make a difference beyond selfish ambition tend, to ignite movements and bring about lasting change.

We now know through the fifth-dimension model that God-size dreams—God-size visions—that transcend self often require courage, resilience, and a willingness to challenge the status quo. They may involve taking risks, confronting obstacles, and overcoming adversity, in pursuit of a greater purpose.

At first glance, God-size dreams can seem grandiose to the extent that they portray personal ambition or even arrogance. Was that not the case with Joseph? As we celebrate his exit from prison and newfound position in a palace, we can easily deduce that accessing such a magnificent opportunity, with all its power and splendor, was indeed the fulfillment of a dream. It wasn't.

What were Joseph's dreams, then? In one dream, Joseph and his brothers were binding sheaves when suddenly his sheaf rose and stood upright while his brothers' sheaves gathered around his sheaf and bowed down to it. In his second dream, he saw his eleven brothers as stars and his father and mother as the sun and moon, all bowing down to him (Genesis 37). Nothing about those dreams project humility, does it? As a matter of fact, his family had a difficult time processing these interpretations because they seemed so far-fetched and self-centered. Such was the case that they launched Joseph into the dimension of betrayal.

Joseph's dreams may have seemed grandiose until we begin to see their fulfillment. The truth is, that the previous four dimensions have changed Joseph. He does not look the same as the seventeen-year-old boy who had the initial dreams. He does not act the same way as when his brothers last saw him before selling him as a slave. He no longer talks the same. His environments through each step of the journey have molded him into the person who was now given access to the palace.

///

I am convinced that God-size dreams change people.

///////////

Is that not like our journey? I am not the same person I was thirty years ago before traversing the very dimensions I have alluded to in this book. My looks have not changed much, or at least I want to convince myself that they haven't. (I think I am in denial about my aging process.) But I can certainly tell you that my thought processes, my skills, communication, and even many of my interests have completely changed. Why? I am convinced that it is because God-size dreams change people. Is the change physical? For Joseph, it was—he looked different, he sounded different, and he carried himself differently because he had been sold into a different culture that had changed everything about his physical appearance. So much so that his brothers did not recognize him. For most, it is the changes in behavior, vocabulary, desires, actions, emotions, and priorities that make you look different.

As Joseph stood in the palace, his demeanor, persona, and overall appearance was a testament of his journey. So, if accessing such a majestic place was not the fulfillment of a dream, then what was? To answer that, we must understand what transpired with Joseph.

Joseph had been summoned out of prison because the king—Pharaoh—had had multiple dreams he could not interpret. To his despair, none of his wise men or magicians had been able to interpret his dreams. Yet, the chief butler, whose dream Joseph had interpreted while in prison, was a living example of Joseph's ability to accurately interpret dreams. Similarly, to his demise, the chief baker had also experienced the interpretation of his dream, which sadly, included losing his life.

When the chief butler became aware of the king's dilemma, his conscience was pricked, and he remembered his grave mistake. Upon his release from prison, he had forgotten Joseph, the one who had interpreted his dream. Fortunately, the time was ideal for him to make it right. He quickly spoke to Pharaoh about Joseph's ability to interpret dreams.

It is no coincidence that by divine providence—a credit Joseph attributes only to God—Joseph not only interpreted Pharaoh's dreams, but he also offered a strategy about what to do. Considering that the interpretation of the dream called for seven years of abundant resources in the land, followed by seven years of scarcity, Joseph's plan would preserve resources for the seven years of famine.

The king needed to execute the plan and did not need to look any further—Joseph would be the commander-in-chief. After all, Joseph had a strategy for dealing with the challenges the country would face over the next fourteen years.

Joseph's strategies and wisdom did not derive from his own intellect.

This is where false humility must take a back seat. What do I mean by that? Joseph could have said, "No! Not me! I don't have the experience to manage such a large endeavor!" He could have said, "How about if I shadow someone?" or "I don't have the qualifications to manage a country's resources." It was not the time to scale back in doubt, fear, and trepidation. The truth is, whether he acknowledged it or not, he had spent the previous thirteen years preparing for that moment. His brothers' betrayal had catapulted him into a palace which helped prepare him for that moment. Potiphar's wife's accusation that landed him in prison served as a blessing in disguise, whereby his management skills were refined.

I have said from the beginning that God-size dreams require God-size strategies and intervention. If this is true, and I believe it is, then we must note that Joseph's strategies and wisdom did not derive from his own intellect. This was a partnership with God. Joseph surrendered to the process, and God met his every need. This should help us understand that when we submit to *our* journey, we do not have to have it all figured out. As we embark on and trust the process and remain open to growth and learning, God will endow us with the necessary strategies, knowledge, and wisdom to see the dream to fulfillment.

What about you? What have you been preparing for? Maybe you are now emerging out of your comfort zone and daring to dream God-size dreams. Perhaps a God-size vision is stirring within you. If so, know that each dimension you face will serve as preparation for the fulfillment of those dreams. Each dimension, regardless of how difficult, will equip you to experience the fullness of your vision. When the time comes, do not scale back in fear, doubt, or false humility. No! You have been created to experience the fulfillment of

God-size dreams. You have been created to experience the fullness of God-size visions.

Ultimately, Joseph's interpretation of Pharaoh's dreams became a reality. Joseph was appointed as the second-in-command to Pharaoh! That alone speaks to our earlier discovery—the fulfillment of God-size dreams will always exceed our expectations. What will Joseph do with all that power? Will he use it to take revenge for the betrayal he has experienced time and time again? Will he use it to amass wealth? To answer *yes* to those inquiries is to limit his God-size dreams to self-aggrandizing behavior. No! Whether he asked himself this question or not, I would imagine that he had to introspectively consider, *Whose dream is it, anyway?*

I know! I know that the initial dreams still linger as grandiose and self-serving. And it seems as if Joseph now had the power and position to see the fulfillment of those dreams in a way that would make him superior. But nothing is further from the truth. His call to administer resources is not self-serving. Within his scope of leadership is the ability to help people through years of famine, to the extent that people would travel from other regions in search of food.

Therein lies the juxtaposition of his initial dreams and their fulfillment. Yes, his brothers traveled to Egypt where Joseph had risen to power. As they appear before Joseph and do not recognize him, they bow down. There it is! Joseph's dreams have finally become a reality, not as an isolated event but as part of a much bigger picture.

Joseph's entire journey—his initial dreams and the subsequent dimensions he traveled through—has boiled down to this single moment. The fulfillment of his dreams, although manifested accurately, has become part of a more profound narrative. Joseph now had to decide between his personal emotions and his God-size fulfillment. As a human being, he could have said, "This is my moment! I am in control! My brothers will pay for what they have done!" Who knows, he may have thought it. Nevertheless, the question, "Whose dream is it, anyway?" should compel him to choose a course of action. Will he allow his grueling past journey and emotions to inform his decision, or will he act based on his present condition and the opportunities he has been given? Will he act based on his pain, or will he act based on his purpose?

Joseph's monologue within the biblical text beautifully captures the answer to those questions. It beautifully captures the meaning and essence of each dimension in a collective and cohesive manner. When Joseph is moved to compassion and can no longer hide his identity from his brothers, he exclaims:

> *I am your brother Joseph, the one you sold into Egypt! And now, do not be distressed and do not be angry with yourselves for selling me here, because it was to save lives that God sent me ahead of you. For two years now there has been famine in the land, and for the next five years there will be no plowing and reaping. But God sent me ahead of you to preserve for you a remnant on earth and to save your lives by a great deliverance. So then, it was not you who sent me here, but God. —Genesis 45:5-8 (NIV)*

Whose dream is it, anyway? The response to that question changes everything. Joseph had every right and reason to celebrate his newfound position of authority. He had every reason to display his power over his brothers. In doing so, his display of power would be an accurate representation of his initial dreams. Joseph must understand, however, that the ultimate fulfillment had more to do with purpose than a destination. He had to acknowledge that his dreams were not something he had personally conjured up but rather, something he had been called to do.

We must realize that while our dreams are deeply personal and reflect our individual journeys, their true significance lies in their ability to transcend the boundaries of our own lives. As we learn from Joseph, dreams that are rooted in empathy, compassion, and a commitment to collective progress, have the power to inspire, unite, and transform societies. They have the power to change families and relationships. They have the power to change us, as dream carriers.

I would be remiss if I didn't point out the obvious. Perhaps it is not obvious but rather hidden in plain sight: the fulfillment of God-size dreams includes the person receiving the dream. That is obvious. It is the dreamer who will experience the fulfillment of a dream. However, as we observe Joseph's calling, we could also consider him a conduit through which a country would be spared destruction. Yet, that was not the full picture either. The fulfillment of the dream, with all its position, benefits, status, and wealth, included the dreamer, but Joseph was not only the recipient of the benefits of that assignment, he was also the carrier.

I point that out because I have encountered countless miserable individuals. They do things in life, work in various positions, and fulfill what they deem is a calling but are miserable. They almost feel forced to do what they do and justify their current status by claiming that they do it for the greater good. They say things like, "Well, I am just doing it for my family!" or "I am not happy, but I am making the sacrifice for God!"

When I consider both of our protagonists' lives, I also think about countless other people I know or have met who have also benefitted personally from the fulfillment of their God-size dreams and visions.

You may ask, "Didn't you say that the fulfillment of God-size dreams should only impact future generations?" No! I have suggested that the fulfillment of God-size dreams extends beyond personal gratification. We don't dream God-size dreams at the expense of an unfulfilled life. On the contrary, it is a both/and approach. We endure the dimensions and enjoy the fulfillment. Like a woman carrying a child for nine months, we carry the weight of the dream, and we enjoy its growth and birth. Like Joseph, we become the recipient of the fulfillment and the administrator of it in a way that impacts others.

The distinction between the third dimension of taste and the fifth-dimension, speaks to this paradox. Using Joseph's example, both places he found himself in looked similar. They were both grand. Both owners were wealthy. Both placed Joseph in a position of power. However, in the dimension of taste, Joseph was the only recipient of the benefits that came with his position. Conversely, in Egypt, although similar to the dimension of taste, he *and* his family were the recipients of the benefits attached to his position. Had he settled for the dimension of taste, he would have missed out on the greater impact associated with the fifth dimension.

24

FORGETTING THE PAIN

"If pain must come, may it come quickly. Because I have a life to live, and I need to live it the best way possible."
—Paulo Coelho

Ever felt stuck? The kind of *stuck* that creeps in because of past emotions? One moment, you are perfectly fine, basking in the fulfillment of your God size dreams, and moments later, you are reminded of past hurts. The memories alone attempt to impede your progress and paralyze you. What do you do?

Celebrating the fulfillment of God-size dreams does not exempt you from painful memories. It is at this crossroads between what is and what was, that your choices will make a difference. Will you press forward in fulfilling your God-size dreams—and experience the fullness of your God-size vision—or will you scale back in doubt, guilt, and shame, only to sabotage your progress and all that is in store for you?

The fifth dimension is about fulfillment! It is about seeing, experiencing, and living in what was once just a taste. It is about witnessing the fulfillment of your God-size dream unfold before your very eyes. It is also about fullness, like with Abraham, whose fulfillment of his God-size vision was not a one-time event but rather a level of fullness that extended past his lifetime. Living in the fifth dimension causes you to appreciate how you endured every other dimension. It is the pinnacle of some very difficult climbs where you look out onto the horizon of your life and declare, "It was all worth it!"

However, I have met, counseled, and mentored an enormous number of people who, at the peak of their lives, have come to a paralyzing crossroads due to past pain. A relationship that reminds them of their past, something someone did, or a painful memory they cannot overcome, brings their progress to a screeching halt.

None of us can negate that pain. Whether physical or emotional, it is an inevitable part of the human experience. It manifests in various forms. We can experience it as loss, heartbreak, failure, or even physical injury, that can leave us feeling overwhelmed and distraught and cause us to question the fairness of life. Yet, amid the agony and despair, pain holds the potential to transform into profound lessons that shape our future selves and guide our actions in ways we may have never anticipated.

Why would we regress by mistaking the fifth dimension for the fourth dimension? Precisely! If we are not careful, what should have remained in the past, can come back, repopulate, and attempt to arrest our progress in the fifth dimension.

Imagine if our protagonist Joseph had not dealt with his pain, betrayal, lack, and years of apparent obscurity. What would have become of the surprise visit from his brothers? I think there is a deeper principle found in a previous statement I made in an earlier chapter. That is, the fulfillment of God-size dreams will always exceed our expectations. Let me show you what I mean.

Embedded in Joseph's narrative between his dimension of obedience and dimension of fulfillment, a story emerges that can be easily overlooked. According to Joseph's own words, his painful journey becomes his shield against the backdrop of past pain. What Joseph is about to experience becomes a reminder that his past can no longer control his future.

> **The truth is, it is often easier to bury the pain and hurtful memories under the proverbial carpet than deal with the healing process necessary to become whole.**

As Joseph rises to power, so do the benefits that come with his new position as second-in-command, the governor of Egypt. The once seventeen-year-old boy who has endured the kind of hardship that would send others spiraling down a vortex of depression is now standing in the middle of a palace with a signet ring on his finger, a gold chain around his neck, and donned in fine linen garments. He was about to use his leadership skills for one of the most meticulous, complex, supply chain management endeavors that any country had experienced. There was only one problem. He had yet to face his past.

What would happen if, without warning, amid his greatest moments of success, his past pain, betrayal, and anger surfaced in ways he did not know how to control? What if it affected his leadership? Would he lack the necessary trust to build meaningful relationships?

The truth is, it is often easier to bury the pain and hurtful memories under the proverbial carpet than deal with the healing process necessary to become whole. Have you heard the adage, "Hurt people hurt people?" I have seen it play out one too many times. Hurt people sometimes exude a defense mechanism as an attempt to shield themselves from experiencing similar hurt.

Here is the good news! It does not have to be that way! Your God-size dream is too great! It is too great to allow your past to interrupt your future.

So, how does Joseph move forward in overcoming his past in a way that would prepare him for the visit of those who betrayed him?

Amid all his success during seven years of plentiful resources, he and his wife had two sons. Wait a minute! Why does that matter? What do Joseph's two sons have to do with the mental and emotional therapy that would help heal him from his past? I am glad you asked!

//

You can't fix your past, but you can set new standards for the future!

//////////

In biblical times, the birth and naming of children was extremely significant. It was not unusual to name a child to solidify a message from God, communicate an affiliation with Him, or (please don't miss this), indicate a new beginning or new direction in a person's life. This was precisely the case with Joseph. He named his firstborn Manasseh, which means "God has made me forget all my toil and all my father's house" (Genesis 41:51, NKJV). He named his second son Ephraim, which means "God has made me to be fruitful in the land of my affliction" (v. 52, NIV).

Until now, the only experience with family, spelled betrayal and hatred. Perhaps, his attempt to get acclimated into the household of the family who had initially brought him in as a slave came to a screeching halt because of the owner's wife's false accusation. But now, Joseph gets a chance to change the dynamics of everything he has ever known. He does not have to pass down his pain to the next generation. His past does not have to dictate his future.

Every time Joseph looks at his son Manasseh, he is reminded, *You have been given the chance to start new. Don't bring the pain of your past into your present. This is* your *family now, your new beginning. You can't fix your past, but you can set new standards for the future!* Every time Joseph looks at his son Ephraim, he is reminded, *Although you are not in your homeland enjoying the warmth and affection of your father who loves you dearly, you have been blessed beyond measure in the very land where you were a slave.*

This ability to recognize both the healing of his past hurts *and* how far he had come from a place of obscurity, pain, and lack, prepared him for an encounter with his brothers. What could have destroyed him became a distant memory that no longer affected his actions. His pain became forgiveness.

When the opportunity to be vindictive arrived, he replaced it with compassion. When his brothers betrayed him, did they not sit nearby and eat their lunch after throwing Joseph into the dry well? In contrast to their behavior, instead of enjoying the abundance of his promotion and leaving his brothers to starve, he sat them at his table because his actions and decisions came from a healed heart.

What do you think would have happened had Joseph held on to pain and allowed it to fester? Like unattended weeds, could it have grown out of control and hindered his ability to show compassion? I often tell people to be careful what they feed. I remind them, "If you feed it, it grows; if you starve it, it dies!" Isn't that like most areas of our lives? A relationship—"If you feed it, it grows; if you starve it, it dies;" a senseless desire, covetousness, or pride—"If you feed it, it grows; if you starve it, it dies!" You get the point. Like many of us, I am convinced that if Joseph had allowed the pain of betrayal to fester, he would have become cynical and untrusting, and, who knows, he may have even burned bridges along the way.

Joseph's sons provide a metaphorical parallel to the fulfillment of God-size dreams in our lives. Oftentimes, we erroneously wait for the right moment, the right time, the right city to live in, the right job, or the right conditions, before we thrive. What if the Giver of your God-size dreams can prosper you where you are despite the adversity you experienced along the way, like what we saw with Joseph? All along, Joseph learned to thrive in adversity.

//

Do not allow your past to interrupt your future.

//////////

As a slave in Potiphar's house, he rose to second-in-command. There, he got a taste of his future. When he landed in prison, he was able to thrive. The warden knew he had nothing to worry about with Joseph in charge. Now, Joseph's child would eternally remind him that he could thrive amid adversity.

Have you missed how far you have come because you have been focused on all the pain, struggle, or lack you had to endure? Lack isn't just a state of scarce financial resources. You may be financially stable but lack peace, meaningful relationships, or emotional wholeness. Like Joseph, look at how far you have come. Shift your focus to your proverbial Manasseh—those things in your life that could help you forget the pain of your past, that you should no longer take for granted. Do not allow your past to interrupt your future.

I recently read a quote somewhere (I can't quite recall where) that said, "Bringing up my past is like searching for me at an old address. You might as well keep moving because I no longer live there!" This does not mean you ignore your past. Instead, you become aware that pain could become a powerful teacher. It often forces us to confront our vulnerabilities, weaknesses, and limitations.

When we experience pain, whether it is the loss of a loved one, the dissolution of a relationship, a setback in our careers, betrayal, or failure, we are thrust into a state of introspection and self-examination. This introspection is crucial because it compels us to evaluate our choices, beliefs, and priorities. We will be catapulted to new levels of thinking, if we heed that path of introspection and choose to move in the direction of fulfillment. The things that held you back then, now propel you forward. Your pain becomes an asset instead of a liability.

HUMILITY AND GRATITUDE

I cannot speak for Joseph, but an analysis of his life leads me to believe that he understood the humbling effect pain has on people's lives. How can someone who wielded so much power, demonstrate so much humility? I think it is because his pain reminded him of his vulnerability and impermanence. It prompted him to appreciate the blessings and joys he had missed throughout his difficult journey.

When we encounter adversity or setbacks, we gain a newfound appreciation for the simple pleasures of life—health, love, friendship, and moments of happiness and peace. For instance, individuals who have faced financial hardships often emerge from their experiences with a deeper gratitude for financial stability and security. They learn to manage their resources wisely, cultivating resilience in the face of uncertainty. They become apt to extend a helping hand to others who are struggling.

> **Pain will become a teacher,
> not an adversary.**

What am I telling you? Do not ignore pain. Face it! Embrace it! Learn from it! While pain may be agonizing and difficult to endure, it possesses the transformative power to shape our character, values, and perspectives. So, by embracing pain as a teacher rather than an adversary, we open ourselves to profound lessons that foster growth, resilience, empathy, and gratitude. As we navigate the inevitable challenges of life, may we recognize the potential for growth and wisdom that pain offers. May we emerge stronger, wiser, and more compassionate human beings as a result.

Remember, what you are experiencing or are about to experience transcends your personal limitations. You are not just fulfilling a goal. You are not just checking something off your to-do list. No! You are experiencing or about to experience the fulfillment of a God-size dream. You are experiencing or about to experience the fullness of a God-size vision. Therefore, attacks and challenges will attempt to stagnate your progress. You must ask God for the resilience and bandwidth to transcend every opposition and address those things that will try to sabotage your life. Don't ignore them! Address them. And when circumstances become painful, decide that the pain will become a teacher, not an adversary. The dream is too big—the vision too great—to become paralyzed by your past!

25

READY FOR ANOTHER CYCLE?

"Life does not end with the fulfillment of one dream!"
—C. Olmeda

Congratulations, you have made it! You are witnessing the fulfillment of a God-size dream that seemed to evade you for so long. Yet here you are. If you close your eyes and soak in how far you have come, it should feel surreal. If it is the fulfillment of a God-size dream, it has exceeded your expectations. It should be so awe-inspiring that you ask yourself, *How did I even get here?!*

For many, your pedigree, upbringing, past failures, and perceived limitations would have taunted, "*That* is not for you! That dream is too big! That vision is too great! You are not qualified!" Yet here you are, basking in fulfillment! You're enjoying the fullness of a God-size vision! For some, like Joseph, you didn't ask for the dream!

Yet, God saw you fit to carry such a grand and fulfilling purpose. You were the right person for the position! You were the right person to fulfill what others would have aborted had they gone through what you went through! You understood which dimension you were in every step of the way and did not give in. You did not give up! You knew that the fifth dimension was on its way!

> **Part of the secret to your success is the ability to live generously.**

Many of you have had to rise to new levels of thinking! Your bandwidth has expanded to sustain your new level of greatness. Yet, considering all you have been through, greatness has not provoked superiority but rather humility. You understand that you could not have achieved this dimension in your life on your own. You are here by divine providence. You are here because your God-size dream—your God-size vision—transcended your personal limitations. No one can rob you of your fulfillment! You have paid the price! You have endured, and it is time to reap the reward for not giving up!

Do not fear losing what you have. Like Joseph, you are an administrator and steward of what you have been given. As a matter of fact, live with an open hand. Do not try to hoard. Do not become selfish. Part of the secret to your success is the ability to live generously.

THE SHIFT

While you enjoy the fulfillment of your God-size dream—the fullness of your God-size vision—allow me to shift your focus to a greater understanding of the fifth-dimension model. Thus far, I have illustrated the fifth dimension as a linear sequential model. (See Figure 1.) From the dimension of dream and vision to each subsequent dimension, you have followed the staircase-like process. If I had to use a business term, each step would have been like climbing the rungs of a corporate ladder. Each step got you closer to the fifth dimension.

Figure 1

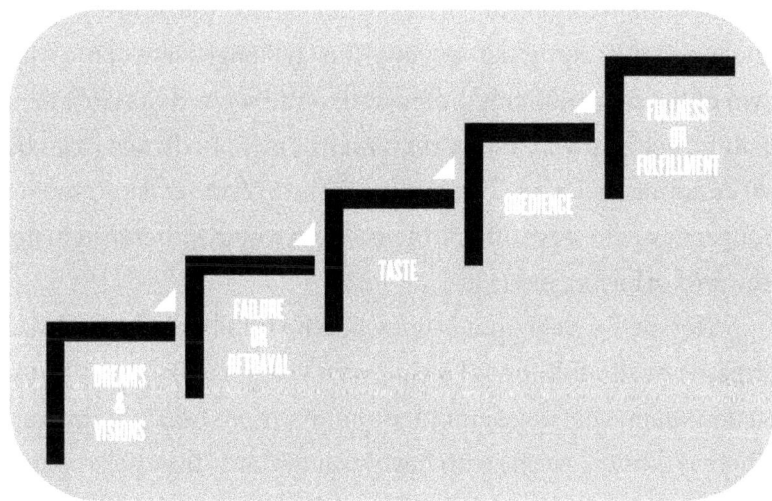

I have used that linear sequential model intentionally. It has allowed me to demonstrate the progression of dreams to help you understand that challenges do not translate to going backward or remaining stagnant. Each dimension was a step in the right direction. Each dimension was an advancement toward the fulfillment of the dream, toward the fullness of your God-size vision.

Here is the challenge. Like in corporate America, adopting the linear model can mislead you to misconstrue the overall objective of the fifth-dimension process as a whole. Like some who have climbed the corporate ladder, they get to the top, enjoy the benefits for some time, and then wonder, *What is next?* Many have climbed the corporate ladder and reached the top only to ask, "Is this it? Where do I go from here?" What happens when living at that level gets old? What happens at retirement age? Do you simply sail off to some tropical island to sip piña coladas by the ocean until it is time to die? Is that all there is?

There is a danger to this linear sequential model once you reach the fulfillment dimension! If we are not careful, the desire to get to the top may become self-serving. The challenges that come with two of the most difficult dimensions—the second dimension of failure/betrayal *and* the fourth dimension of obedience—can be so daunting that when you approach the fifth dimension, you no longer desire to serve others. Instead, you would rather bask in the rewards of having made it.

So let me be clear, that is not what the fulfillment of God-size dreams or the fullness of a God-size vision is all about. Those actions depict personal ambitions more so than God-size dreams. There is nothing wrong with healthy ambitions. They help people strive for achievement or distinction. But ambitions can become unhealthy as well. They can become destructive and inhibiting and lead to greed. That is not what this book is about.

This book has delineated the process of fulfilling dreams and visions that transcend your personal limitations. Getting to the "top" has never been the objective. It has more to do with greatness and impact that transcends you, makes a difference, and carries eternal value. So, if the fifth-dimension model is not linear and sequential . . . then what is it? What happens after you get to the fifth-dimension and experience the fulfillment of your God-size dream? What happens when you get to the fifth-dimension and experience the fullness of the God-size vision you've been carrying? I will tell you! When you get there, you will receive a fresh dream at any moment—a new vision—for the next phase of your life. Let me explain.

THE SPIRAL

The fifth-dimension model is more of a linear *cyclical* model than it is a linear *sequential* model. (See Figure 2.) That means that each dimension you go through is not a step you climb to the top but a growth process that begins with a dream or a vision, that escalates and then repeats—but from a place of greater strength.

Figure 2

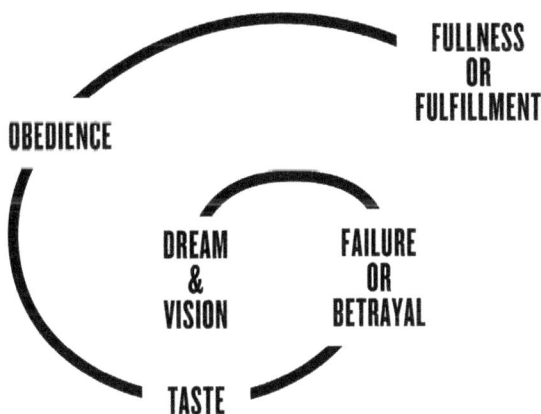

Every part of the cyclical model is important. The starting point denotes a starting point in your life. Consider Joseph, for instance. He was seventeen years of age when he received his dreams. His uninhibited exuberance caused him to divulge his dreams to his brothers which set off the series of events delineated throughout his biblical narrative. As he navigated each dimension, he would not return to his starting point. Instead, he would mature, build resilience, and grow past his initial limitations. Each dimension was an opportunity for growth.

With every dimension you overcome, you carry with you lessons learned. The dimension of failure and betrayal will help you move into the future with newfound wisdom. You did not lose sight of the dream during those difficult moments. Instead, you reevaluated your life and understood how to try again—but with increased knowledge and greater wisdom.

The dimension of taste helped you understand that if it is just a taste, it is only a matter of time before the very things you are tasting run out. The dimension of taste helped you prioritize your life to ascertain whether selfish gain *or* your character and integrity were more important. It helped you to understand that some things are just not worth tarnishing your reputation over. You realized during that dimension that the dream was too great for you to settle there.

The dimension of obedience almost had you. I know! That was a tough one—perhaps the toughest. Those moments of pain, silence, obscurity, and loneliness made you question whether there was really a God-size dream or whether it was a figment of your imagination. The tugging for one more act of obedience had you questioning whether the sacrifice was worth it. But you remained steadfast. You developed selfless behavior. You learned to live with an open hand and not allow people, places, or things to control you. You matured through that dimension to become a more generous, compassionate, and tenacious individual.

In each individual dimension, you may have felt as if you were not making progress. But collectively, you look back over the last four dimensions and realize how far you have come. You are not the same person. You have grown and matured beyond your wildest imagination. Now what?

The current fulfillment of your God-size dream or the fullness of your God-size vision may not be the end, depending on where you are in your life—your age, vocation, or familial status. That would make our model a linear sequential one that ends once you reach the top. Instead, you may get a fresh dream or a new vision for the next phase of your life. (See Figure 3.)

Figure 3

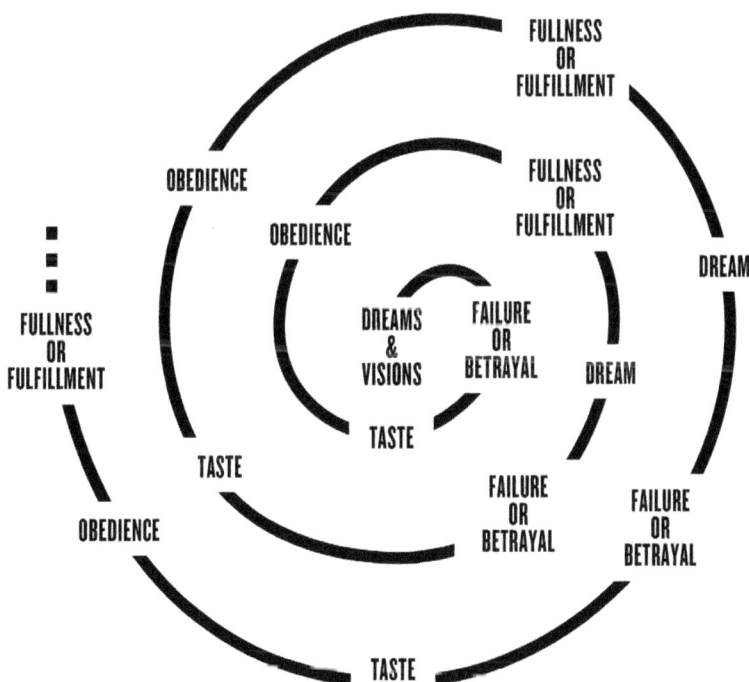

I am reminded of a biblical character by the name of Caleb. He was one of two leaders who had optimistically walked with Moses who led the people of Israel out of Egyptian bondage. It had been forty-five years since God had made him a promise. At the age of eighty-five, he said the following:

> *"I was forty years old when Moses, the servant of the LORD, sent me from Kadesh-barnea to explore the land of Canaan. I returned and gave an honest report, but my brothers who went with me frightened the people from entering the Promised Land. For my part, I wholeheartedly followed the LORD my God. So that day Moses solemnly promised me, 'The land of Canaan on which you were just walking will be your grant of land and that of your descendants forever, because you wholeheartedly followed the LORD my God.'*
>
> *"Now as you can see, the LORD has kept me alive and well as he promised for all these forty-five years since Moses made the promise—even while Israel wandered in the wilderness. Today I am eighty-five years old. I am as strong now as I was when Moses sent me on my journey, and I can still travel and fight as well as I could then. So give me this hill country that the LORD has promised me."*
> —Joshua 14:7-12 (NLT)

For forty-five years, Caleb had carried an unfulfilled dream—a vision of a promised land. He had been part of other God-size dreams, and he had been able to witness their fulfillment. Yet here he was! Years of battles, struggles, pain, and adversity had built him into who he eventually became. And at the age of eighty-five, he was back in dimension number one.

Unlike the corporate ladder, he neither climbed down nor was he demoted. Instead, he grew and matured from years of experience and became ready to take on a new God-size dream.

GENERATIONAL DREAMS

God-size dreams and God-size visions are so powerful that they transcend generations. When they do, they keep the cyclical model spiraling outward through multiple generations. The beauty of that, is that one generation may begin to live out the fifth dimension from the very beginning of the dimension of dreams and visions without realizing that they are fulfilling a dream that was declared before they were born. Let me give you an example.

I can provide you with countless examples of people who have lived out the fifth-dimension model. As a matter of fact, I can assure you that anyone who has experienced the fulfillment of a God-size dream or has lived in the fullness of a God-size vision has not been exempt from any of the dimensions. It is part of the process toward fulfillment and fullness.

Think about the familiar biblical character, Moses. Popular films like the 1956 remake of *The Ten Commandments*,[5] made popular by actor Charlton Heston, or Universal Pictures' 1998 *The Prince of Egypt*,[6] have generated broad familiarity with the general public about Moses's journey. Moses and the people he led out of Egypt—the people of Israel—are a classic example of the fifth-dimension process.

   1) **First Dimension** (Dream/Vision): Moses received a vision—a calling—to lead the people of Israel out of slavery in Egypt.

---

5   Cecile B. DeMille, *The Ten Commandments* (October 5, 1956; Hollywood: Paramount Pictures).
6   Brenda Chapman, Steve Hickner, and Simon Wells, *The Prince of Egypt* (December 16, 1998; Universal City: Universal Pictures).

2) **Second Dimension** (Failure/Betrayal): Although they escaped (not without struggle), they became a rather murmurous and rebellious people while traversing the desert. They failed to follow directions. Moses was betrayed by their criticism and constant complaints.

3) **Third Dimension** (Taste): They got to the border of the Promised Land. Moses sent spies to bring back some fruit from the land. They returned with an abundance of grapes, pomegranates, and figs. Although they enjoyed the fruit of the land, it was only a taste. If they looked up after enjoying the fruit of the land, they would realize they were still outside of the promise.

4) **Fourth Dimension** (Obedience): They had to adhere to every bit of instruction to finally occupy the God-size dream. (Most of the original generation that came out of Egypt, including Moses, never entered the Promised Land).

Please do not miss this! From Moses's perspective, he was living out the first dimension as if he were starting from the very beginning—and he was. But generationally, he was not starting from the beginning. He was continuing the cyclical process that Abraham had started over four hundred years earlier.

When we read about Abraham's God-size vision (while he was still Abram), we read that God spoke to Abram. He said:

> *"You can be sure that your descendants will be strangers in a foreign land, where they will be oppressed as slaves for 400 years. But I will punish the nation that enslaves them, and in the end they will come away with great wealth." —Genesis 15:13-14 (NLT)*

As you can see, our protagonist Abraham endured the fifth-dimension process (the entire model from beginning to end), and the fullness of his God-size vision transcended his life span. Generationally, Joseph, Abraham's great-grandson, endured the fifth-dimension process, as well, and helped save Egypt and countries near and far from famine.

As generations grew and multiplied, we can witness people begin the fifth-dimension process as if it were the first dimension. Unbeknownst to them, they were beginning a process within a larger cycle of promises that had been made years prior.

///

> **You do not go back to the beginning. Instead, you grow from the beginning.**

///////////

What if our God-size dreams—our God-size visions—are the fulfillment of promises made to previous generations? What if they are dreams and promises that were made in or birthed out of the hearts of previous generations, and we have become the recipients of those dreams and visions? To us, the first dimension is the first dimension. But in God's plan, the end has already been declared from the beginning. For Moses, for instance, what he thought was the first dimension—the beginning of a vision—was actually the fifth. Why? Because the outcome of what Moses was about to experience had already been established four hundred years earlier—he just didn't know it.

NEW DREAMS AND VISIONS

As you move beyond the fifth dimension, allow me to alleviate any concerns you may have about starting over. By carefully observing the cyclical model, you will understand that you *do not* go back to the beginning. Instead, you grow *from* the beginning.

There are God-size dreams and visions that are reserved for certain phases of life. Maybe, like Joseph, you received a God-size dream at the age of seventeen and saw its fulfillment years later while you were still young. At that point, know that you have not reached the last step on some ladder and have nowhere else to go. No! You will get a fresh dream—a new vision—for the next phase of your life. Although you will have to navigate each dimension, you will do so with newfound knowledge, wisdom, and resilience.

When you become familiar with the model and understand which dimension you are in, you will live it out with newfound wisdom. The sting of betrayal that may have caused enormous pain during your first cycle through the five dimensions may not sting as badly. If it does, you have learned to deal with it and can move forward to the dimension of taste. You do so confidently, acknowledging that you are on your way to the fifth dimension.

With every cycle, you expand. Your resilience becomes solidified. Your focus becomes clear. Your ability to endure adversity has been tested and tried. The questions and doubts you had throughout the dimension of obedience, during your first cycle, become *aha* moments the second time around. They become moments when you say, "Aha, I know what dimension this is! It is time to serve—to show compassion to others even while I am not being served and feel forgotten." The pain may come, but now you know how to endure it! You now know that the dimension of obedience is the darkest because it is the dimension right before fulfillment.

As you go through each fifth-dimension cycle, know that the timespan between those difficult dimensions—the second dimension of failure/betrayal and the fourth dimension of obedience—may become shorter and shorter. Why? Because you have learned from your past. This is precisely why it is important to implement the lessons that each dimension brings. Don't ignore them. You will need them as you navigate the process of a fresh dream, of a new vision.

You were born to fulfill God-size dreams.

As I leave you ruminating in thought, wondering which dimension you are in or what the next phase of your God-size dreams and God size visions will look like, I will confess something. For me, only one constant common denominator has enabled me to dream God-size dreams and given me strength, resilience, and faith. That is, my complete surrender to my Lord and Savior Jesus Christ (who, by the way, also endured the fifth-dimension process). So, as I live out each fulfillment and bask in the fullness of every vision, I do so, knowing that it transcends my life. I live to serve as the loving demonstration of Jesus Christ on planet Earth. I live acknowledging that my impact, the fulfillment of my dreams, and the fullness of my visions, must outlast my time on earth and impact the next generation.

As you move forward, know that giving up will never be an option. You were born to fulfill God-size dreams. You were born to see the fullness of God-size visions. Whatever dimension you find yourself in today, know that, unequivocally and undeniably, the fifth-dimension is on its way!

CONTINUE YOUR JOURNEY

AVAIL
PODCAST

Printed in the USA
CPSIA information can be obtained
at www.ICGtesting.com
CBHW051922031224
18385CB00007B/104